To Barbara & Elsie,
Best wishes!
Kathryn Zeller 12/24/91

TALK OF THE TOWNS

Stories from Southwest Michigan

Written and edited by Kathryn S. Zerler

Illustrations by Vicky Nemethy

Format by Peggy Lyons Farrington

Sales & marketing by Jennifer Schanze
For information call (616) 982-6739

Published by St. Joseph Today
520 Pleasant Street
St. Joseph, Michigan 49085

Thank you for your purchase of this book.
All proceeds benefit St. Joseph Today, the
promotional organization for the city of St. Joseph.

This book is dedicated to Glenn L. Zerler
who contributed the title, *Talk of the Towns*,
and many hours of patience and proofreading.

Other books by Kathryn S. Zerler

Love Poems for Dreamers
Blended Pleasures
On the Banks of the Ole St. Joe

"Who would want to write a book about the banks in St. Joe?"

Overheard in Majerek's Hallmark-Reader's World near a display of copies of *On the Banks of the Ole St. Joe*.
December, 1990

(...maybe Dick Schanze, Dan Smith, Dick Whiteman, Bill Early, Bob Baldwin, Bill Cole, Jim Giffin, Tom Ricketts or Bob Mylod?)

Preface

Ode to an Old Landmark

Come and sit by my side little darlin'
I've a story that I wish to tell
You've heard of the St. Joe sock foundry
The one they call Cooper and Wells
It's located down on the beach folks
Near a tavern we all knew as Joe's
There's a sign on the side of the building
"The Makers of Iron Clad Hose."

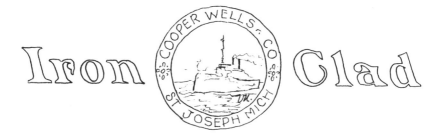

Shortly after receiving a copy of *On the Banks of the Ole St. Joe,* my father, Louis C. Schultz, called and sang this old drinking song to me. (Remember drinking songs?) He said something in the book reminded him of it after all these years.

Many others told me stories about life in St. Joseph, Benton Harbor, Stevensville and the townships. These are their stories.

History is, after all, a series of stories about people.

Kathryn Schultz Zerler
Executive Director of St. Joseph Today
from September 17, 1984 to present

Contents

"Storytelling is the key to learning."
Rene Fuller

"The universe is made of stories, not of atoms."

Muriel Rukeyser

I. Working

The Oldest Profession

Contrary to Hollywood depictions, "working girls" were not glamorous. As evidenced by this photograph of "Popcorn Jenny" (center woman in white) and her "girls," the women were tough cookies. The one in the front, sitting on the left, is actually a man who was their bouncer.

Their house was located near the docks in downtown St. Joseph in the 1890s. The women drew much of their trade from sailors and passengers who arrived on board the large boats which entered the harbor. However, local men were known to frequent the house, too. And "Popcorn Jenny" loved to drum up business—while shocking and annoying local women—by touting her girls around town on rides in open carriages.

Caldwell's Livery and the Caldwell Theater

Jim Caldwell's great-grandfather, J.C. (James Cornelius) Caldwell, came to St. Joseph from Chicago. In the 1880s he built and operated a livery stable at the edge of town, where City Plumbing & Heating now stands.

According to an advertisement reprinted in *The Herald-Press,* Caldwell's Livery had "the finest horses, best carriages and most careful drivers. Satisfaction guaranteed in every respect." Caldwell's was the "carriage repository for the celebrated Courtland wagons and carriages, sold at Factory Prices." He encouraged potential buyers to "give us a call before purchasing. Just the thing for comfort." The ad closed with a statement signed by Jas. C. Caldwell. It said, "I would respectfully announce that I am better prepared than ever to furnish excellent turnouts, having lately added many new and stylish teams to my stock."

When horse and buggies were no longer needed—in about 1915—Caldwell built a movie theater on the site. The Caldwell Theater was the first and only theater in southwestern Michigan for many years. Admission in the 1920s was ten cents.

J.C. Caldwell died in 1925; his son, Elliot Hugh preceded him in death in 1923. The business was left to grandsons, James William and Vernon Edward Caldwell, who leased the theater to Butterfield, Inc. It was sold to Butterfield circa 1942, and was demolished due to fire damage in 1962.

Great-grandson, J.L. (Jim) Caldwell, remembers an annual Caldwell Theater event held once each summer. All kids could get in free for a Saturday afternoon matinee by bringing a dog and parading across the stage. Imagine what a mess that must have been!

Jim Caldwell has lived in the area for 70 years. He was the area manager for the State of Michigan's Corrections Department in the Parole and Probation Division. He currently resides in Stevensville with his wife June.

J.C. Caldwell, born June 11, 1841.

Inside of Caldwell's Livery in the late 1800s.

J.C. Caldwell on a carriage circa 1900.

J.C. Caldwell on a sleigh in December, 1907.

*J.C. Caldwell with
five-year-old J.L. (Jim)
Caldwell in 1925.*

The Ice Cream Cone Invention

Lew Filstrup gave us the scoop on Frank Tarbell, the man who invented the ice cream cone. Tarbell was born in 1877 the son of Charles Tarbell and Antoinette Burridge Tarbell and great-grandson of Sterne Brunson, one of the· founders of Benton Harbor. Tarbell worked as a barker at the Louisiana Purchase Exposition in St. Louis in 1904. His job was to lure people into the various exposition booths.

One day, he noticed a pancake and waffle booth next to an ice cream vendor with neither doing much business. Tarbell got the bright idea of rolling a waffle into a cornucopia shape and adding a ball of ice cream. With his barker's voice, he skillfully enticed the crowd to try his concoction and encountered instant success.

After the fair Tarbell exploited the idea by contacting Lewis Burridge, his cousin who had just graduated from Purdue engineering school. Together they designed a portable oven to roll and bake the cones. The ovens were made in Michigan City and sold very well along with a recipe for batter. Many ice cream shops bought the ovens and Tarbell became a millionaire. Unfortunately he lost it all in the stock market crash of 1929. He died a poor man in 1949 and is buried in the Morton Hill Cemetery in Benton Harbor.

The Electric Motor Car

Lars Larsen Filstrup and Milo Covel joined forces in 1890 and formed the Covel Manufacturing Company. In 1904 Covel's stock was purchased by the Filstrup family. Fourteen patents were issued to the company before 1908 especially in the areas of sharpening, stretching, brazing and conditioning saws for saw mills. The company prospered as its products were accepted by major mills in the country.

In 1912 the Covel Manufacturing Company of Benton Harbor formed a subsidiary called the Covel Motor Car Company. The company designed and built two electric motor cars. The cars were owned by the two sons of Lars and Anna Erikson Filstrup, Eddie C. and Alvin W. Filstrup.

Mrs. E.C. drove one car and Mrs. A.W. drove the other. Top speed was 10 miles per hour and the driving range was about 20 miles. Huge batteries were located in the trunks of both cars and mercury rectifiers kept in the Filstrups' garages were plugged into the cars every night to recharge the batteries.

Lewis L. Filstrup, son of Belle and Eddie C., recalls his mother driving him and his siblings, Nancy and Edward, to Jean Klock Park from their home on Pipestone Avenue in Benton Harbor. He remembers that the car's batteries didn't always make it all the way home and they would have to wait by the side of the road for the batteries to recuperate enough to finish the journey.

Production plans for the electric cars were abandoned in about 1914 when gasoline powered automobiles became popular.

Lewis L. Filstrup joined Covel Manufacturing Company in 1935. He became president circa 1955. His sister is Nancy Clark, a Berrien County Commissioner.

One of the two electric motor cars produced by the Covel Manufacturing Company in 1912.

Practical Jokes

Ruth Gillespie Grootendorst tells about a prank her father Frank pulled in 1906 or 1907 with business neighbor and good friend, Henry Richter, who co-owned the Richter & Achterberg Hardward Store at 218 State next door to Gillespie's Drug Store. As the story goes, the men decided to liven up the town with an elaborate practical joke.

They worked 12 to 14 hours every day; their customers became their friends, and their work was their life. Practical jokes—dreamed up during slower working hours—were their favorite form of recreation.

First, they checked a fictitious character into a hotel. Next, they wrote a despondent suicide note which they put into the pocket of a man's suit. Gillespie and Richter surreptitiously left these items along with a straw hat and a woman's photo in a disheveled heap at the end of the south pier near Silver Beach. The woman in the photograph was a "flora-dora" girl with a big hat; her slim waist was cinched-in with corsets. The imaginary man was supposed to have done himself in over an unrequited love affair.

When the note, photo and clothing were first discovered, the pranksters had a good private laugh. However, they began to get worried when they looked down from the bluff and witnessed the U.S. Coast Guard fervently dragging the lake and river. The young men swore each other to secrecy and were never caught.

The papers got hold of the story and tried—without success—to locate relatives of the man or the woman or both. The local paper wrote a flowery front page story of the despondent lover ending it all with strains of amusement park music grinding out in the background.

* * *

While Gillespie and Richter were still bachelors, they and some other eligible young men in town made a pact that the first one of them to get married would have to ride a donkey down State Street.

When Gillespie moved to town, he resided at the Lakeview Hotel on the southeast corner of Ship and Lake Blvd. Sometime after he moved in, a sharp looking 18-year-old from Chicago named Helen Shoden came to work as a hostess in the Lakeview's dining room. Gillespie saw her there and fell in love.

One day, Shoden walked past the window as Gillespie was getting a shave and a haircut in Dr. Burton's barber chair. Gillespie told the barber, "That's the girl I'm going to marry."

But he was afraid to buy her a ring because he didn't want to be the one to ride the donkey. It is not known who among the bachelors had to finally consummate the promise.

Frank T. Gillespie arrived in St. Joseph in 1905 and bought a drug store which became Gillespie's Drug Store at 220 State Street. The site has been a drug store since 1866. He married Helen Shoden in 1907. The couple had six children, Collins, Ruth, Thomas, Robert, Richard and William.

Collins, Robert, Richard and William all became pharmacists like their father. Ruth worked in the drug store for many years and remembers her father's subtle sense of humor.

When a customer came into the store and asked Frank if he would buy his deceased brother's wooden leg for resale in the store, Frank asked, "Is it embalmed?"

The man looked puzzled. Frank continued speaking with a straight face, "Is it the right leg or the left?"

Ruth had to walk away to keep from laughing out loud.

Frank bought the leg, and later Ruth found a purpose for it when Joe Killian called needing a good birthday present for Clell "Doc" Johnson. They decided to give him the hollow leg filled with liquor bottles. The leg was later seen sticking out of trunks of cars, dressed up with shoes and socks, and reclining in other unlikely places.

12

Gillespie Drug Store (St. Joseph, Mich.) stepped up business with this new Liquid Fountain

The Gillespie Drug Store soda fountain.

*   *   *

Ruth remembers working at the soda fountain with her father when Art Poinier, Ed Brown and Doc Johnson paid a messenger to send Frank several insulting telegrams every few minutes. The three pranksters were sitting at the counter—holding back their snickers—enjoying sodas while they watched Frank read each telegram without looking up and quietly pocketing the insulting remarks.

CONGRATULATIONS
JITTER AND I HAVE BEEN
WANTING TO CONFER ONE
FOR A LONG TIME
ART

Art Poinier, who operated a studio over Gillespie's Drug Store in the 1930s, drew this cartoon of Frank Gillespie.

Bill Gillespie relates another time when his father—knowing that Bob Carlton had been called away from his store and would telephone in the late afternoon to check up on things—called the innocent clerk working at Carlton & Walters and told him not to use or answer the telephone between three and six o'clock that afternoon because the phone company was "blowing out the telephone lines."

The clerk followed the authoritative businessman's directions and didn't touch the store's three telephones all afternoon even though they rang several times. The clerk also wrapped up the telephones in bags tied with rope as he had been instructed to do. Finally, Carlton—who had called many times as expected—ran frantically to his shop—located then on the west side of the 200 block of State Street and later on the northwest corner of Broad and State—to find out what was wrong.

Carlton knew he had been the object of yet another harmless prank when the young clerk said, "The telephone company called and told me they were blowing out the phone lines."

*   *   *

Even the service clubs got into the act in those days. Bob and Ruth Gillespie were both part of a skit enacted at a Kiwanis Club meeting held at the Whitcomb Hotel. In a script written by Emil Tosi, Ruth portrayed a notorious gangster moll, Virginia Hill, who was always in the news. She was interrogated about the identity and whereabouts of her boss by the likes of Bob Gillespie portraying "Sen. Gillespie," Emil Tosi portraying "Sen. Kiwaniser alias Rudy Halley-Tosi," Fritz Stueland portraying "Sen.

Stueland," and Homer Banks, a shy businessman who Ruth embarassed when she jumped onto his lap and identified him as her "gangster boss and lover." Ruth remembers they were all laughing so hard, tears ran down their cheeks.

* * *

In late 1918, Lou Upton and Frank Gillespie celebrated the end of World War I by hauling wooden piano crates from Schoeneberg's Music House to the middle of State Street. They set fire to them, creating a monumental bonfire to "the war to end all wars."

Schoeneberg's Music House...

Frederick Schoeneberg moved his family to St. Joseph in 1914 and opened the first music store in town. Schoeneberg's Music House was located on State Street and handled pianos, musical instruments, radios, sheet music and related supplies. Schoeneberg also tuned pianos, and later added appliances to his stock. After thirty years of business in St. Joseph, Schoeneberg closed the store in 1942. His granddaughter, Margie Schultz Ball, fell heir to the plaster of Paris fruit and vegetables used for displays inside the refrigerators. Remembering those days, she said, "How lucky my dolls were, they never knew all the food I served them was pretend."

* * *

Collins and William Gillespie continued the tradition of good clean fun when the sidewalk was torn up during the State Street renovations of 1979. The two pharmacists buried a time capsule near the entrance to their drug store. The capsule is located about eight feet from the door and two feet north.

It contains items such as a Susan B. Anthony dollar, a newspaper and a Timex watch. When asked why they went to all the trouble to assemble the capsule, Bill said, "We wanted to see if the watch would keep on ticking."

William G. Gillespie was involved with the renovation of downtown St. Joseph through his seat on the St. Joseph City Commission. He began his term in 1974, and was elected mayor—a position he currently holds—in 1990.

Lucker's Meat Market

The building that now houses Chan's Garden Restaurant at 310 State Street was the home of Lucker's Meat Market in the early 1900s. The butchery had sawdust covering the floor and was well-known in town for fine meats personally cut and trimmed by its owner, Fred Lucker.

One afternoon, when the other downtown merchants weren't busy—but Lucker was—they decided to pull a practical joke on him. The merchants took turns calling Lucker on the telephone and hanging up.

Lucker & Sons at 310 State Street; L. D. Huber is seated with the dog, Fred Lucker is standing on the right.

The incessant ringing of the crank-type telephone agitated Lucker. He began to use rather colorful language as he shouted into the telephone for the pranksters to cease.

One caller posed as a representative of the telephone company and said, "Mr. Lucker, we'll have to remove your telephone if you continue to use such violent language."

Lucker replied, "I'll do it for you!" With that, he ripped the phone off the wall and threw it onto State Street.

Fred Lucker was the father of 17 children. Information for this story was supplied by his youngest son, Ted Lucker, who resides in Stevensville with his wife, Elaine.

Demise of a State Street Bridge Tender

When the Graham & Morton steamer *City of Holland* pulled into the port of St. Joseph shortly after 4:00 a.m. on July 11, 1913, its signal for the State Street bridge to swing open went unanswered. When the whistle was repeated, it again went without a response. The steamer was making its way closer to the bridge and quickly shut down its engines to avoid a collison with the structure.

Police officer Hugh O'Hara was notified. As he hurried to the bridge, the officer felt that something was very wrong. Climbing into the bridge tower, O'Hara found the night tender, Robert Ludwig of 911 Harrison Avenue, slumped in a chair with his head bowed as if in sleep. O'Hara shook Ludwig's body to awaken him, but the form was lifeless.

The body was taken to the Baitinger & Kingsley morgue where an examination by physicans determined that death by heart failure had occured approximately one half hour before the steamer entered the harbor. Justice Collier impaneled a coroner's jury composed of John Bruley, Martin Burkey, Frank Gilbert, William Simmons, Fred Hess and Chris Rill.

Mrs. Arthur F. (Leona) Ludwig submitted this story about her father-in-law. Robert Ludwig was born in Germany in 1878 and came to this country with his parents when he was three years old.

The Longner Farm

In 1918 most of the property where the Orchards Mall now stands was farmland owned by Dr. Frank King Sr. Fred Longner lived with his parents on a seven-acre farm at the corner of Pipestone and Napier. Many memories prevail from those days. There were many chores as the animals and food were brought down from a farm near Sodus. Longner cultivated the cornfield which is now Orchards Mall with a one-horse cultivator.

Longner had a pet lamb which followed him all around and he would have to play tricks on the lamb or it would follow him to school. The lamb played "butting" by pushing with its head. It became quite agressive as it grew older. One day, as Longner's father was bent over the fence pouring food in the pig's trough, the lamb came up behind him and butted him head first over the fence into the trough. The kids had to squelch their laughter since Longner's father did not find this funny.

Another pet was a tumbler pigeon that was so tame it would sit on Longner's shoulder as he worked in the garden. "We used to throw that pigeon up in the air and watch it flip around. The pigeon liked it, and we had a lot of fun," Longner recalled. "I remember one of the neighbors had a donkey which two or three of us would ride at a time. When the donkey tired of playing with us, he would put his head down and we would slide off."

Stealing melons was popular with teenagers when Longner was young. He went with his friends to his father's patch. "I told them not to ruin the vines, and that I had left big ones in a certain place," Longner said. "My father would hear us and come outside with a big spotlight and we would run. He would have given us as many as we wanted, but the fun was in getting away with something."

Another pastime was dropping from rafters in the barracks where cattle were kept. Some of the neighborhood kids drove the animals underneath the rafters where those who were hanging dropped on their backs. Longner said, "Oh boy, we were off for a hilarious ride until we were bucked off."

He went to work without pay in the Gilmore Brothers Furniture Store during the Depression. "I needed the experience, and in 1929 there wasn't much else to do," Longner said. "It turned out that I was a pretty good salesman and they hired me to work on Saturday afternoons and evenings for $2.50. I could speak German, and that was an advantage with some of the customers."

Fred Longner *resides in a home he built with his wife Alberta on the south end of the property on Pipestone. The Longners celebrated 60 years of marriage June 27, 1991.*

23

Why Was the Road Named Pipestone?
...Georgia Atwood looked into the matter. She talked to a lot of people including two Potawatomi Indians and several history buffs, but no one seemed certain of the name's origin.

One source said it was named after a soft, red stone that local Indians used to fashion peace pipes called "calumets." Someone else described this stone as "hard, dull red or mottled pink and white." The book, *Michigan Place Names* by Walter Romig, says the banks of Pipestone Creek contained the best clay for fashioning pipes. Another source thought there had been a large stone near the road which resembled a pipe.

The Green Cottage Restaurant

Popular with many people around St. Joseph and Benton Harbor was the Green Cottage Restaurant, long renowned for good food and drink. Located on Lake Michigan at the north end of Ridgeway, the Green Cottage was originally built in 1930 in what was then Benton Township. The property was annexed to St. Joseph in 1976 and zoned residential.

In the beginning, the restaurant was one room built by Martha and Joseph P. "Porky" Harvey. The interior included a bar, one restroom and a kitchen. At that time, the Harveys leased the property with an option to buy.

They started the restaurant there in 1930 to feed the WPA (Works Progress Administration) workers who were building the brick road that is now Ridgeway Drive. The Harveys regularly served noon meals for 20 to 30 workers. The menu consisted of ham sandwiches and draft beer at 25 cents each.

Green Cottage drawing by Ron Heyn.

Later, as business grew, the Harveys added a dining room, and her mother, Lorraine Memmler, came to cook for them. Known to everyone as "Ma," Memmler came to this country from Norway at the age of 16.

With "Ma" in the kitchen, Martha Harvey was free to act as hostess and cashier. "Porky" tended the bar, and the business grew. The Harveys named it the Green Cottage Inn and advertised it as "on the beach in St. Joseph, Mich."

By the mid-1930s the Green Cottage Inn touted "mixed drinks, properly concocted" and chicken, fish and steak dinners for $1.50. The menu offered a steak sandwich for 35 cents, and on Friday nights the Harveys held a special fish fry for 15 cents.

Still later, the Harveys added a three-room apartment to the structure and lived there until the business sold in the 1940s. Their green and white placemat depicted a map of the area including routes to the restaurant from St. Joseph, Benton Harbor and the Twin Cities Airport. Despite the prime location, the Green Cottage Inn was not a tourist attraction and remained a local favorite through the years.

The white frame, Cape Cod style building had awnings on the front and side entrances and shaded windows all around. The parking lot could accommodate three or four rows of cars and was located on the south side, but many Ridgeway and Higman Park residents walked to the restaurant.

The Green Cottage Inn also had a finished basement with inside and outside staircases. The basement, paneled with knotty pine, contained walk-in coolers and a small bar.

During World War II practice drills for air raids were a common part of life. In a drill, all businesses were supposed to close, all visible lights extinguished, and all cars were to be off the streets. Blackouts were meant to prevent raids on the city by enemy bombers.

When air raid drills occurred "Porky" Harvey would take his customers into the basement and serve drinks there "on the house" until the blackouts were concluded. It was rumored that gambling by local volunteer "air raid wardens" took place in the basement bar.

Chuck and Doris Miller owned it from the late 1940s to 1954 and called it Miller's Green Cottage. A one-time partner of the Millers, John Globensky recalls that "you could get a good steak for $7. My brother, Richard, and I used to eat there, and in a young and foolish moment we thought we could make a lot of money in the bar business." So, for a little more than a year, the Globensky brothers, both attorneys, were restaurateurs.

"We even held some of our bar meetings there," said John Globensky. "It was a nice place with tables in the dining room and booths in the bar. It attracted mostly local traffic."

For Allen Klemm, the restaurant was one of the nicer ones for its time. "When Chuck and Dory Miller were the proprietors, we ate there every Sunday night. I used to order the salmon and the swordfish steaks. And we also often went there for lunch. We spent a lot of time at Grant Blacken's Sportsman's Port on the north side of the

St. Joseph River. We took our breaks at the Green Cottage."

Allen Klemm and his boating friends traveled approximately a mile and a half down North State Street to the Green Cottage. North State Street is now Upton Drive, and Sportsman's Port, once a small bay of boat docks, is now the LaFarge Corporation.

During the late 1950s, the Green Cottage was owned by Mort and Grace O'Rourke.

Lila and Joseph Blake owned the restaurant from 1961 to 1965 and called it Blake's on the Lake. By then it had changed hands four times and had a history of good food and a friendly atmosphere.

Once inside the wide main entrance on the south, customers walked immediately into the lounge where there were booths to the left and right. A white brick fireplace was on the east wall of the bar, and the kitchen was to the north.

"We were surprised to find beautiful hardwood floors in the bar," said Lila Blake. "It was a friendly place but not elegant. The building was so old that if the wind blew too hard or from a certain direction, I knew just where the sand or the snow would blow in."

The building had French doors facing Lake Michigan and a little porch with small windows on the lake side. The porch was used for year-round dining. Bigger windows were in the dining room, but they overlooked the parking lot.

"In those days, people didn't think of dining with a view as they do now," recalled Eileen Globensky. "The restaurant itself was little and dark. It had a small bar with booths, and a small porch facing the lake."

"If you stood up, you could see the lake. But when you were sitting at the tables, the lake could not be seen over the ridge," said Blake. "I could see the lake from my office which overlooked Jean Klock Park, and the view was wonderful."

Blake remembers that the building was surrounded by dune grass and cottonwood trees. "Those trees used to drive me crazy," she said. "Some days in summer the cotton puffs blew around so much it made it look like it was snowing. But the sunsets were different every day and I loved working there."

The dune grass and the cottonwood trees are still there. And a small rock garden covered with sedum has been restored and maintained and still flourishes next to a hardy spirea bush at the base of an old brick pillar near the edge of the property. The pillar now denotes the boundary line between St. Joseph and Benton Harbor, and is also the northern property line of the lot.

The building was demolished on July 6, 1971.

A private home was built there in 1981. In keeping with the beachscape environment, much of the original landscaping from sedum to spirea was maintained along with the most dominant vegetation, dune grass.

The Empire Center, Circa 1930s

Gwenn Ueck Schadler recalls the hub of activity in her neighborhood as the "Empire Center," a nickname given to the shops on the corner of Empire and Broadway in Benton Harbor.

According to Schadler:

"Anyone living in the area from Pipestone to Colfax and from Britain to May Street had to 'run' almost daily to the Empire Center for something. We walked over for a prescription at Bizer's, filled by Ted Bizer, or a coke at the fountain served by his sister, Ella. We picked up bread at Golkas Grocery where Mr. and Mrs. Golka took care of us.

In the evenings we would find an excuse to go to Olds Dairy—a quart of milk or an ice cream cone—because everybody hung around Olds at night.

On Fridays and Saturdays, my mother bought meat for our Sunday dinner at Baumeisters from Mr. Steinke. Biederbecks Bakery was across from Baumeisters. There, we picked up rolls and coffee cake.

I took the bus, which stopped at Bizers (coming from Fairplain) each morning about eleven o'clock, to my job in St. Joseph. At night, I took the last bus and sometimes didn't get home until after eleven. I tell you, I was so scared to walk from the bus to my home in the 900 block of Columbus, but somehow I did it. There was really nothing to be afraid of, except the dark, because I knew everyone along the way."

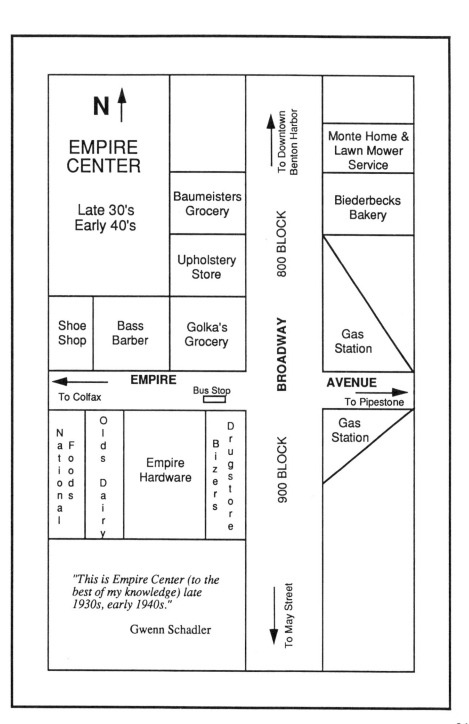

N ↑

EMPIRE CENTER

Late 30's Early 40's

Baumeisters Grocery

Upholstery Store

Shoe Shop

Bass Barber

Golka's Grocery

To Downtown Benton Harbor

800 BLOCK

BROADWAY

Monte Home & Lawn Mower Service

Biederbecks Bakery

Gas Station

EMPIRE

AVENUE

To Colfax

Bus Stop

To Pipestone

National Foods

Olds Dairy

Empire Hardware

Bizers Drugstore

900 BLOCK

Gas Station

"This is Empire Center (to the best of my knowledge) late 1930s, early 1940s."

Gwenn Schadler

To May Street

Whitcomb Hotel Memories
from Irma F. Harris

Irma Harris tells about her family's tenure at the Whitcomb Hotel which her husband, Leon J. Harris, managed from 1934 to 1964.

When St. Joseph celebrated the 100th anniversary of its incorporation in 1934, the city's centennial banquet was held in the Whitcomb. Mrs. Harris remembers the affair being so large that tables were set up in the lobby clear to the registration desk. Mr. Harris, as the hotel's new managing director, was scheduled to be on the program. He wrote a speech and rehearsed it many times; finally getting it down to one paragraph. When called upon at the banquet, Harris merely stood up and shyly took a bow. Later, Harris became an accomplished speaker.

*   *   *

One quiet Sunday evening, Mrs. Harris was walking to the Marquette Lounge when she noticed a man watching an artist who was painting a mural on the wall of the stairwell leading down to the Marine Bar. When he turned to look at her, she recognized him as the notorious bank robber and killer, John Dillinger. Mrs. Harris nonchalantly continued walking to the lounge. A lone woman was there who she knew as the wife of a distributer of the *Chicago Examiner*. Mrs. Harris told the woman that Dillinger was in the lobby. "Gott In Himmel!" the woman exclaimed.

Then Harris walked to the registration desk and whis-pered to Irving Hallet, the assistant manager, that Dillinger was in the hotel. He said she was mistaken, the

man was a salesman from Grand Rapids named Hitler
who had been in the hotel before this time.

Several years later, Mrs. Harris read a biography of
Dillinger. It said that twice he had been in a hotel in St.
Joseph, Michigan.

SULPHUR SPRINGS
St. Joseph , Michigan

LEON J. HARRIS
Managing Director

Some famous people who visited the Whitcomb were Fran Allison, Ann Landers, Duke Ellington, Eleanor Roosevelt, Dr. Margaret Mead and the violinist, Rubinoff. Eddie Fisher and Debbie Reynolds came when they were newly married.

Some permanent residents of the Whitcomb were Jane Cutler, Madame Billie Shepard, Ethel Higman, Waldo Tiscornia and Carrie Upton.

* * *

The Harrises' apartment in the hotel had a beautiful view of the St. Joseph River and the lighthouse on the North Pier. The master bedroom was located on the northeast corner facing the river and the alley.

For weeks, city garbage collectors drove through the alley at five o'clock in the morning. Rattling cans and talking loudly, the men disturbed the Harrises and their guests in the hotel.

Leon Harris complained to the city manager, Leland Hill, many times without results. One morning, exasperated from being rudely awakened again, Harris called Hill at five in the morning and said, "I thought you'd like to know that the garbage men are here."

The noise ended.

* * *

The Shepard and Benning Company of St. Joseph and Paris, an exclusive women's clothing store, was on the southwest corner of State and Pleasant Streets during the early to mid-1900s. The store was owned and operated by Madame Billie Shepard (as she liked to be called). Shepard purchased original fashion designs in Paris and brought them to St. Joseph.

Madame Shepard lived at the Whitcomb. Mrs. Harris remembers her apartment as quite elaborate with gold cornices installed at the windows; her French furniture was upholstered in pettipoint.

Shepard and Benning organized style shows, and Mrs. Harris said it was an honor to take part in them. The shows always started with swim suits and ended with a bridal party. One spring, Madame Shepard asked Mrs. Harris if her then eight-year-old daughter, Gloria, could take part in a style show wearing a dress identical to one that had been designed by Shepard and Benning for that year's blossom queen.

Mrs. Harris said,"No."

Shepard was indignant. "Why not?" she insisted.

"Because she has the measles," Harris replied.

*   *   *

Another source, Ruth Gillespie Grootendorst, recalled that Jane Cutler lived at the Whitcomb when Madame Shepard did. The two women were great friends and regularly took their evening meal together in the dining room. They requested the same waitress every night.

One evening, that waitress was off duty and the women were served by a waitress-in-training who was having a difficult time. As the meal went on, the waitress became more and more frustrated. Finally, dinner was over and the waitress could see the end in sight. She asked the women if they cared for dessert.

Mrs. Cutler said no, but Madame Shepard requested a demitasse.

The waitress stormed out of the dining room and into the kitchen. Once there, she exclaimed, "That's it. They called me a damned ass! I'm not waiting on them anymore."

* * *

Irma and Leon Harris

Mrs. Harris remembers many political candidates visiting the Whitcomb. When G. Mennen "Soapy" Williams was a young man, he not only shook hands with all of the guests, he went into the hotel kitchen and shook hands with every employee there—even the dishwashers. Then, Williams walked outside and shook hands with everyone in the downtown stores. His efforts paid off when he was elected governor of Michigan.

G. Mennen "Soapy" Williams campaigning in Gillespie's Drug Store with Collins Gillespie.

One spring, when Leon Harris was chairman of a short course on hotels at Michigan State University, Duncan Hines and Otto Eitel (managing director of Chicago's Stevens Hotel—later the Hilton) stopped at the Whitcomb to have lunch. They were on their way to East Lansing to speak at the seminar. Duncan Hines remarked then that he would like to return to the hotel for a vacation.

Soon after, Mr. and Mrs. Duncan Hines spent a week at the Whitcomb. The Harrises spent time with them everyday and the foursome became friends. Mrs. Harris remembers taking them to Gillespie's Drug Store for one of the "famous" chocolate sodas. The two couples continued to meet every year at the American Hotel Convention.

Mr. Hines said word-of-mouth is the best advertising, and that good coffee will bring people back. He mentioned the Whitcomb in his book, *Adventures in Good Eating*. After 25 years of being listed in his book, Hines sent the Whitcomb a silver plaque inscribed with the words "For Excellence in Food and Service."

* * *

During World War II, Mrs. Harris was in charge of selling War Bonds for the hotel. She had a desk set up in the lobby for this purpose, and remembers that negotiable bonds—which could be cashed anytime—were her biggest seller.

At one point she had sold more than half a million dollars worth of bonds on the Sixth War Loan. Nelson Foulkes, a reporter for the *Herald-Press,* encouraged her to "try for a million next time."

Each bond drive lasted six weeks. The motto for the Seventh War Loan was "Bring the Boys Home." For this drive, Harris helped his wife with strategies to raise more money and attempt to reach the million dollar goal. He suggested that she go outside the hotel and solicit industries.

When she sold Lou Frankel of Cooper & Wells fifty thousand in bonds, he said, "Come back if you can double it."

Waldo Tiscornia of Auto Specialties purchased one hundred thousand; H.B. Ross of Ross Carrier bought another hundred thousand; Stanley Banyon of the *News-Palladium* bought thirty-five thousand. As promised, Frankel purchased an additional fifty thousand.

To raise even more funds, the Whitcomb held a War Bond Banquet and offered a free ticket to anyone who purchased a one thousand dollar bond. Mrs. Harris fondly remembers the gala banquet held in the Tropical Room. "The room was decorated with a large American Flag in back of the speaker's table," she recalls. "A statue of liberty was the centerpiece, and war posters ran along the skirting. The long tables in the room were appointed with paper dolls depicting people in military uniforms. We had chicken on the menu as meat was rationed."

The banquet was a huge success. Mrs. Harris sold an estimated two hundred thousand dollars in bonds, but she thought she wasn't going to reach her goal.

She drove to Producer's Creamery. They asked, "Where have you been?" When Producer's purchased thirty-five thousand, Harris' total reached one million twenty-three thousand and she became Michigan's first place seller.

County Bond Chairman, Austin R. Maujer of the Maujer Publishing Company on Ship Street, sent Harris an invitation to an awards dinner. She said, "I will never forget the letter that began 'To my star of stars salesman.'" At the dinner, which was held in the Whitcomb's St. Joseph Room, Mrs. Harris was awarded a silver medal for her work. It was a stag dinner and she was the only woman there.

*   *   *

Mr. and Mrs. Harris dressed for dinner every night. If he was ready before her, he would go downstairs. On one such evening, after Harris had gone downstairs, he decided to start their dinner with avocados California style.

Some avocados had been sent from California and were stored in a walk-in refrigerator in the basement. Harris went inside, leaving the door ajar. The avocados were in a carton at the back of the large cooler. Just as Harris was bending over the carton, the light went out and the door slammed shut. An employee had noticed the door ajar and closed it thinking someone had carelessly left it open. The light was switched off from outside the cooler.

Harris was trapped inside for several minutes before anyone heard the ruckus he raised. Needless to say, all of the refrigerated rooms were immediately equipped with inside door handles and light switches.

Leon Harris served as president of the Michigan Hotel Association, was on the state committee for the Mackinac Bridge, was the first president of the Twin City Chamber of Commerce, a planning director for Memorial Hospital, and was one of the first directors of the Community Chest. He believed that citizens should help the community in which they made their living.

Note: *Read* On the Banks of the Ole St. Joe *for more information on the Whitcomb.*

The Wells Field Skating Rink

Thelma Troost recalls the winter of 1935-36 well. She was pregnant with her son, Peter, and had trouble sleeping. Many times in the night she would get up, turn on the lights in her home at 2019 South State, make a pot of coffee and do some light housework.

At the same time, Walter Sauerbier was working across the street turning Wells Field into an ice skating rink. A painter by trade, Sauerbier had extra time in the winter and volunteered to flood the field and operate the rink for the city. He was given use of a fire hose and all the water he needed. The task was an arduous one, and Sauerbier often stayed at the rink all night, sometimes for three and four nights in a row.

Knowing the Troost family, and seeing their lights on, Sauerbier took to stopping in for coffee in the middle of the night. Using the Troost house as a kind of office, Sauerbier frequently telephoned St. Joseph's Water Department—also in the dead of night—and shouted at them for more water pressure. Later, with the rink completed, he brought injured children to the Troosts for bandages, warmth and a bit of tender loving care. Toward the end of the season, Sauerbier held a field day with games and races. He gave prizes which he solicited from local merchants.

Peter Troost was born on March 12, 1936. Thelma and E.J. Troost have a daughter, Barbara G., and have lived in St. Joseph since 1929.

* * *

Jean Dalzell adds this story about her father, Walter Sauerbier...she says, "My grandfather, Charles Sauerbier, was chief of police in 1904 and 1905. One day someone came into the station and told him that his son—my father—was diving off the mast of one of the big boats in the channel. Grandfather went to the channel and yelled at him to come down.

"My father replied, 'O.K. Dad, I'll be right down.' And off he dived."

Walter Sauerbier

Frank Lloyd Wright's Ego Revealed

Years ago, Frank Lloyd Wright was here building a home for Howard and Helen Anthony on Miami Road in Benton Harbor. Charles O. Zollar was scheduled to transport the architect to an undisclosed destination in an airplane owned by Air Craft Components, a company owned by Zollar and his wife, Babe. As he was about to board, Wright scrutinized the plane and said to Zollar, "Is this airplane safe?"

Zollar assured the architect that it was.

Wright, who was 90 years old at the time, continued, "Of course you realize that you have the future of modern architecture at stake."

Zollar coolly replied, "Something more important than that is at stake here—my own life." With that, Zollar slid into the pilot's seat, started the engines and off they went.

The Zollars owned Aircraft Components in Benton Harbor. Charles O. Zollar was a Michigan State Senator from 1964 to 1978. Howard Anthony purchased Heath Company in 1935 and moved it from Chicago (where the company was founded in 1926 by Edward Heath) to Niles, then to Benton Harbor, and then to St. Joseph. Anthony died in a plane crash in 1954.

Charles Zollar

Tom Dewhirst and the POWs

During World War II, Tom Dewhirst was appointed as an advisor to the local War Manpower Commission. He suggested using Prisoners of War for harvesting, processing and storing agricultural products.

Given the general shortage of workers, this practice spread across the entire nation after Dewhirst received a letter from President Roosevelt asking him to request volunteers from the Grant Prisoner of War Camp near Rockford, Illinois. Dewhirst presented Roosevelt's letter to the camp's commander and—to everyone's amazement—nearly all of the German prisoners volunteered. Arrangements were made for a train to transport 387 prisoners to the Benton Harbor Naval Armory where they were lodged for a year.

The House of David and the Welch's Grape Juice Company guaranteed to pay the government the prevailing wage of 50 cents a day per laborer under the terms of the Geneva Convention. A committee from the Geneva Convention twice visited the area and toured the House of David Cold Storage Plant.

The House of David Cold Storage Plant

Tom Dewhirst designed the first automatic barrel stacker for use in the House of David Cold Storage Plant. Clark Equipment Company patented it and built it. The stacker did the job of seven people who formerly had the arduous task of stacking heavy barrels of food by hand. The stacker opened up a new phase of material handling in the food industry.

Dewhirst managed the cold storage and processing plants where the House of David froze and stored more than one million pounds of fruit daily during the 1930s. They were the first to freeze many products in 1932. They packed and froze asparagus, rhubarb, strawberries, cherries, red and black raspberries, boysenberries, blackberries, peaches, plums, apples and grapes.

They were the first to discover that placing grape juice in a 32-degree cooler would maintain the color and flavor of the juice as well as settle the tartrates. They worked with the American Can Company to develop a lacquer that could withstand the acids in grape juice, and they were the first to market grape juice in cans.

H. Thomas Dewhirst is a past president of the Benton Harbor and St. Joseph chambers of commerce, served on the Michigan Agricultural Marketing Council, was appointed Commissioner of Agriculture by Governors Romney and Milliken, was president of the Twin Cities Area Development Corporation, founded and was president of the Fruit Belt Chapter of National Association of Practical Refrigerating Engineers, is a past president of Blossomtime and holds an honorary, lifetime seat on their board of directors.

Memories of Western Union

Gwenn Ueck Schadler recalls fond memories she has of a one block area in downtown St. Joseph on Ship Street from Lake Boulevard on the west to State Street on the east.

From 1942 to 1946, Schadler came to work from Benton Harbor on the Enders Bus Company, bus #309. She hopped off the bus at the corner of Ship and State where the Tip Top Cafe was located. Bill Connors and others ran the Tip Top and allowed her to charge all of her food by the month.

After her morning coffee, Schadler crossed the street to the Peoples State Bank. Working inside were tellers Cleo Swan and Doris Nuechterlein who always had a smile or a funny comment for her. Schadler often saw John Stubblefield, then president of the bank, who referred to her as "daughter" (along with many others) as she passed through the bank to her job at Western Union which was located next door.

This was war time and Schadler's hours were 11:00 a.m. to 9:00 p.m. It was her job to close the office and deliver personally the terrible telegrams from the War Department which read, "We regret to inform you that your son..." This assignment was especially difficult for her because she usually knew the families of the servicemen.

All local corporations did their business by telegrams. Each day Schadler spent time working with the 1900 Corporation (now Whirlpool), St. Joe Machines, Auto Specialties, Theisen Clemens, Boating Industry and Truscott Boats.

Alma Knight was the manager of the St. Joseph Western Union, and her husband, Harold Knight, ran the Benton Harbor office. Schadler worked alone from 3:00 to 9:00 p.m. with alternating messengers, Mary Slattery Deleeuw and Carl Diener, who delivered telegrams—save for those from the War Department—on foot or by bicycle.

Postal Telegraph was just down the street, north of the Tip Top. Jean Gilbert was manager. A great rivalry existed between Postal Telegraph and Western Union. When Western Union bought out Postal in 1943, all Western Union employees received big bonuses. Schadler remembers buying a watch from Peacocks in Chicago, three pieces of matching luggage, and a white sewing machine (which she still owns) with her bonus money.

Next to Western Union was the License Bureau, then St. Joe Loan, the alley, and the elegant Whitcomb Hotel where the coffee shop was always full of locals and guests. Across the street from Western Union was Burkhard Brothers General Store, located on the south side of Ship Street where the Peoples State Bank's parking lot is now. Schadler remembers the two brothers sitting out front in chairs, talking to everyone who walked by. They sold a variety of items to locals and to tourists—popcorn, peanuts, postcards, cigars.

Kittycorner from Peoples State Bank was Bakers Ice Cream where June Heppler Selent worked. She and Schadler became friends, and Schadler said, "Whenever I wanted to get a message to her, I sent her a telegram by messenger. Our biggest decisions were to choose whether we were going to dance at Shadowland Ballroom at Silver Beach or Crystal Palace at Paw Paw Lake or Ramona at Sister Lakes or even if we had enough gas to go to Indian

Lake near Dowagiac. It took 25 cents to fill the tank to get to Indian Lake."

Gwenn Ueck Schadler has lived and worked in the twin cities for 68 years. She married Harold Schadler in 1946.

Gwenn Ueck Schadler standing in the window of the Western Union office in downtown St. Joseph. The sign says "Wires for War! No more messages of felicitation or congratulation after December 21st, 1942."

Sheffield Drug Company

Elowyn Ann (Stephenson) Keech supplied us with the following list of requirements for rural school children. She said, "I can still see the sun coming from somewhere high above my head while I stood deep in that book-lined canyon waiting with Daddy to pick up the required books. Does anybody remember that wonderful wood-cabineted drug store? Did all rural school children in the county have to drive there? Coloma students certainly did! These prices will never be seen again...nor the 3% sales tax. I must have been in Kindergarten, which was not for socialization way back then, but a real, live class."

* * *

List of Text Books and
Authorized Requirements

FOR THE

Rural Schools

OF

Berrien County

STATE OF MICHIGAN

—

1942 - 1943

—

FOR SALE BY

Sheffield Drug Co.

132 Pipestone St., Benton Harbor, Mich.

School Supplies

—

Pencils	3 for 5c—3 for 10c—5c
Ink Tablets	10c
8 Color Crayons	10c
Mechanical Pencils	25c—50c—$1.00 and up
Pencil Tablets	5c—10c
Fountain Pens	25c-$1-$2.95-$3.95-$5.00
16 Color Crayola	15c—25c
24 Color Crayola	25c
Water Colors—8 Color	25c—35c
Loose Leaf Note Book	10c—29c—39c
Note Book Paper	5c—10c
Colored Pencils	5c—10c—15c
Ink	10c—15c
Paste	5c—10c
Scissors—Blunt or Pointed	10c
Compass	15c
Rulers	5c—10c
Chalk—Dustless 70c	Soft—40c
Note Books—All Sizes	5c—10c
Spelling Tablets	5c—10c
Manilla Paper—per ream	90c
Colored Paper—All colors—per pkg. 50 sheets 25c	
Zipper Note Books	$1.49—$4.89

50

Prices on New Books for the Rural Schools of Berrien County

BEGINNERS AND GRADE I

Before We Read 32c
We Look and See 24c
We Work and Play 24c
We Come and Go 28c
Work-Book for Pre-Primer 28c
Fun with Dick and Jane .... .68c
Work-Book for Fun with Dick and Jane 28c
Our New Friends 80c
Work-Book for Our New Friends 28c
Webster Arithmetic Tablet No. 1 ... . 20c

Pencil, tablet, crayons, scissors, paste, eraser

GRADE II

Webster Arithmetic Tablet No. II 20c
New Curriculum Number Bk. Grade 2 .... 44c
Friends and Neighbors 87c
Work-Book for Friends and Neighbors 28c
More Friends and Neighbors 87c
Work-Book for More Friends and Neighbors 28c
Spelling—Progressive Word Mastery 28c
Writing; Economy-Primary 30c—Palmer 15c.

Pencil, tablet, crayons, scissors, paste, eraser

GRADE III

Elson-Gray Basic Reader-Book III 84c
New Curriculum Arithmetic Bk. I 91c
English in Action—Lower Grades $1.06
English in Action—Practice Bk. M. 28c
Spelling—Progressive Word Mastery 28c
Writing; Economy-Primary 30c—Palmer 15c.
Pencil, tablet, crayons, scissors, paste, eraser, ink, pens, penholder.

GRADE IV

Elson-Gray Basic Reader-Book IV 91c
Spelling—Progressive Word Mastery 28c
Atwood Thomas Geog. The Earth & Its People-Lower Book $2.09
Atwood Thomas-Work Book in Geography 28c
Writing; Economy-Intermediate 30c—Palmer 15c.
New Curriculum Arithmetic-Bk. I 91c
English in Action-Lower Grades $1.06
English in Action-Practice Bk. N. ... .28c
Pencil, tablet, crayons, scissors, paste, eraser, ink, pens, penholder.

GRADE V

Elson-Gray Basic Reader-Book V .` 91c
New Curriculum Arithmetic Bk. II 91c
Spelling—Progressive Word Mastery ...., ... 28c
English in Action—Middle Grades $1.10

Plus 3% Michigan Sales Tax
Book Prices Subject to Change Without Notice

English in Action—Practice Bk. O. 28c
Atwood-Thomas Geog.-The Earth & Its People-Lower Bk. $2.09
Atwood-Thomas Work Book in Geography 28c
Burnham & Jack History-The Beginnings Of Our Country 99c
Writing; Economy-Intermediate 30c—Palmer 15c.
Webster Dictionary for Boys & Girls $1.36
Winston Simplified Dictionary For Schools $1.48
Pencil, tablet, crayons, scissors, paste, eraser, ink, pens, penholder.

GRADE VI
Elson-Gray Basic Reader-Book VI 91c
New Curriculum Arithmetic Bk. II 91c
Spelling—Progressive Word Mastery 28c
Atwood-Thomas Geog.-The Earth & Its People-Higher Book ...$2.24
Atwood-Thomas Work-Book in Geography 28c
Burnham & Jack History-The Growth Of Our Country .... .99c
Winslow-Healthy Living-Book I 95c
Writing; Economy-Advanced-30c—Palmer 15c.
Webster Dictionary for Boys & Girls $1.36
Winston Simplified Dictionary For Schools $1.48
English in Action-Middle Grades $1.10
English in Action-Practice Bk. P. 28c
Pencil, tablet, notebook, paste, eraser, ink, pens, penholder.

GRADE VII
Elson Junior Literature-Book II $1.03
New Curriculum Arithmetic Bk. III 99c
America-Our Country-History $1.67
Spelling—Progressive Word Mastery 32c
Atwood-Thomas Geog.-The Earth & Its People-Higher Book .. .$2.24
Weed, Rexford & Carroll-Useful Science-Complete Book $1.52
English In Action—Upper Grades $1.14
English In Action-Practice Bk. II 36c
Writing; Economy-Advanced-30c—Palmer 25c.
Webster Dictionary For Boys & Girls $1.36
Winston Simplified Dictionary For Schools $1.48
Pencil, tablet, notebook, paste, eraser, ink, pens, penholder.

GRADE VIII
Elson Junior Literature-Book II $1.03
New Curriculum Arithmetic Bk. III 99c
Spelling—Progressive Word Mastery 32c
Fundamentals of Citizenship-Mich. Edition $1.25
English In Action-Upper Grades $1.14
McClave-Outline of Michigan Civil Government 33c
Weed-Rexford-Carroll-Useful Science-Complete $1.52
Williams Word Study-Orthography 33c
Writing; Economy-Advanced-30c—Palmer, 25c.
Webster Dictionary For Boys & Girls $1.36
Winston Simplified Dictionary For Schools $1.48
Pencil, tablet, notebook, paste, eraser, ink, pens, penholder.

Keech is also the founder of Fog Horn Records & Tapes, a
company which has twenty-two and one-half minutes of
St. Joseph's old diaphone fog horn in its archives and for
sale. The diaphone horn existed on the North Pier from
1934 to 1970. Following is Keech's account of how its
resonance was preserved and her company was born:

*"Well maybe not every hostess, while waiting for her
dinner guests, tapes a rain storm. But it was such a
wonderful spring rain. Warm and coming straight
down...the windows didn't need to be closed. So I set
up the stereo mikes and recorded it, just for fun, and
while the tape was running the old diaphone about a
half mile away began to sound and naturally that
added to the mood.*

*"Not until later that spring of 1970 did I realize I had
a special tape. The Coast Guard replaced our old
diaphone with the present electronic signal (aka dog
whistle) and eventually neighbors and friends asked
to hear the tape.*

*"My son challenged me in 1985 to make it available
to people and that is how Fog Horn Records & Tapes
was born. Rob had taken about a million photos of
the North Pier and one worked beautifully for the
cover. Ken Parr, now of CBS-TV but then of KP
Recording, re-mixed to eliminate the wind and other
undesirable sounds.*

*"I remember telling Ken I had no idea how many of
these tapes would sell, but my mother could be
counted upon to buy three. And she did. Many other
people bought it, too. Some without connections to
St. Joseph, but with a love of that sound. Mystic*

Seaport has carried the tape in their catalog for several years, and many lighthouse museums on both coasts use it to illustrate the sound that they too have lost."

Diaphone Fog Horn
1934-1970

Elowyn Ann Keech is a member of the Institute of Business Designers. She is a certified contract interior designer, and a professional affiliate of the western Michigan chapter of the American Institute of Architects. Keech is also owner of Edgewater Club Annex, a small apartment building near Lake Michigan that is listed on the State Register of Historic Sites.

Gertrude Brown

Beginning in 1942, Virginia Handy remembers her weekly trips to Gertrude Brown's small, stucco-covered house at 424 East Britain Avenue in Benton Harbor as more than an introduction to music.

"I would walk into the living room where Mrs. Brown was seated at the Baldwin concert grand, finishing up a lesson with another pupil, and I would pick up a book such as the poetry of Kahlil Gibran or an illustrated history of ancient Greece and Rome or Will Durant's *Story of Philosophy*. She let her students borrow wonderful books and records," Handy said. "She was an introduction to great literature and to great minds."

Handy fondly recalls the drills and methods employed by Brown in teaching music basics such as the scales and chords, use of a metronome, slow practice and the singing tone. "She had her own method for teaching sight-reading," Handy said. "We learned the notes on the treble clef lines by memorizing **E**very **G**ood **B**oy **D**eserves **F**udge; the notes in the spaces were **F A C E**.

On the bass clef, the notes on the line were **G**ood **B**oys **D**eserve **F**udge **A**lways; the notes between the lines were **A**ll **C**ows **E**at **G**rass."

Handy remembers Brown saying, "My students are like my own children." Brown worked with hundreds of children for more than fifty years. She recognized the value of music to childhood development and understood individual differences and special problems.

"None of Gertrude Brown's piano students or friends will forget her," Handy said of the woman who died on June 1, 1976 at the age of 80. "When she died, the *Herald-Palladium* wrote an editorial describing her as 'a great lady who will be truly missed by young and old alike.' She coached 14 students to win two-week scholarships to the National Music Camp at Interlochen sponsored by Monday Musical Club. I won for piano in the first competition in 1950, along with Bonnie Batek for violin. Clarys Butgereit won in 1951, and the winner in 1952 was Robert Murphy who I remember as a talented little boy whose legs barely reached the pedals. Now he's an instructor of piano at Interlochen."

Through her association with Brown, Handy was part of the monthly Sunday Music Club. She recalls, "Performances by gifted musicians such as Joan Faber, pupil of Alice Baran Hatch, and Josephine Iannelli Brummel, a pupil of Clara Kennel and now a concert pianist, gave the twin cities a rich cultural experience. Another unforgettable person was Emery George, who emigrated from Hungary in 1946 and became a professor of German literature at Princeton University."

Gertrude Brown was born in Ames, Iowa on December 4, 1895. After graduating from the Chicago Conservatory of Music she came to Benton Harbor in 1918 to dedicate the new organ at the Methodist Peace Temple. There she met Dr. W.E. Brown who she married in 1920. Dr. Brown served as mayor of Benton Harbor for one term in the 1940s.

Gertrude Brown, May 22, 1976.

Viewpoint

In 1947 Tom Lyons went to work for the Ross Carrier Company which was owned and operated by founder H.B. Ross and his sons Harry, Don, Malcom and Buster. Lyons' position was assistant steel buyer under Bob Lewis. Harry Ross, as the head of purchasing, was their boss.

After Lyons had worked in the company for an appropriate period of time, Ross called him into his office to tell him that he was doing a good job and deserved a raise in pay. Lyons stood frozen to the floor not knowing what to say.

Sensing his employee's shock, Ross opened a small cabinet in the corner of his office and pulled out a bottle of Old Forester whiskey. "Now," Ross said, "we'll have a drink to seal the deal."

Stammering for words, Lyons said, "Old Forester...that's good whiskey."

Ross replied, "Ain't no such thing as bad whiskey, some's just better than others."

Thomas E. Lyons lived in southwestern Michigan for 36 years and now resides in Las Vegas, Nevada with his wife Elenore.

Carroll Crafts

Dale and Marian Hogue opened Carroll Crafts in 1949 with high hopes and about $500 worth of merchandise. That winter their store at 807 Main Street in downtown St. Joseph was so cold Marian hung thick fabric over the brick walls to keep warm.

The next year they moved the business to 505 Pleasant Street where they remained for 35 years. They've sold tableware, baskets, gifts, women's clothing and accessories, picture frames, notecards and seasonal merchandise such as Christmas items. In the store that was named after Dale's middle name, the Hogues have seen and heard it all.

"I want to tell beginning retailers to hang in there, look at the bright side, enjoy your customers and your work," Dale says with confidence. At the age of 80, his step is full of determination. "Don't get discouraged," he says. "I think we took in $45 the first week and then business fell off."

Carroll Crafts moved to 218 State Street in 1985 which gave them more space, so they opened a series of smaller shops in the back and called it the Galleria. In the summer, the store was open from 10:00 a.m. to 10:00 p.m. seven days a week and drew a strong following from tourists. "If more retailers would do that, St. Joseph would have a whole new industry," says Dale who once strapped a pedometer to his belt and learned that he walked nine miles inside the store in one day.

With business going strong, the Hogues decided to close the doors on Carroll Crafts in 1991. As the oldest single-

owners and operators in retail, the Hogues have been among the most progressive. Downtown St. Joseph will miss them.

Excerpts from the
"Diary of a Tired and Retired Retailer"
by Dale C. Hogue

Monday, Jan. 14, 1991: In our 42 years in business, just received the 337th request for a contribution from the Fire Fighters Union. I have sponsored more wrestling matches than ESPN.

Tuesday, Jan. 15, 1991: Just had the 221st leak from the apartment above the store on our new clothes. Landlord said he just repaired that same leak only two weeks ago with chewing gum.

Wednesday, Jan. 16, 1991: Just received our 3,000th call for a door prize. This one was from the Sunday Horse Riders Association.

Thursday, Jan. 17, 1991: Local lawyer called to say he is representing a woman who stubbed her toe on our entrance. After some conversation he asked what I was going to do when we closed Carroll Crafts. Told him I was studying to be a lawyer.

Friday, Jan. 18, 1991: Please no more calls from the newspaper and the shopper for ads in their special supplements before the rates go up!

Saturday, Jan. 19, 1991: Woman trying on dress today could not get the zipper down. Wanted the dress for half price or would call the rescue squad.

Monday, Jan. 21, 1991: Same woman called today to ask if we would call her back when the $100 dress went down to $22.50. Be sure to call her at home or at work. Has answering machine.

Tuesday, Jan. 22, 1991: Placed ad in local paper, "For Sale: flame thrower only used to keep candles lit on Moonlight Madness nights."

Wednesday, Jan. 23, 1991: Michigan Sales Tax representative called and would like to review our tax records. Must have all sales slips, cancelled checks, invoices, etc. in his office by 10:00 a.m. tomorrow morning. Wants to review and check years of 1961, 62, 63, 64, 65, 66, 67, 68 and 69. Has cousin in the truck rental business.

Friday, Jan. 31, 1991: Yesterday was my first day of retirement. Could not sleep last night because I kept worrying about the fact that I had nothing to worry about.

A Secret Meeting at the Whitcomb Hotel

Tom Sparks tells a political story from the 1950s. Sparks had been a city commissioner for several years. As an incumbent up for reelection, he remembers one campaign as being particularly hectic. "The opposition was terrible," he recalls. "We had to hold secret meetings to plan our strategy."

One such meeting was planned for the Whitcomb Hotel. Leon Harris, hotel manager, was a staunch supporter of the established government and happy to lend space for the meeting.

As local merchants, doctors, bankers, lawyers and other downtown business persons were contacted, it became apparent that the size of the group would be close to 100. Harris said that was no problem; they could use the solarium which was located on the seventh floor and equipped with 17 sunlamps so hotel guests could enhance their suntans. The room had cushioned chairs, so everyone would be comfortable.

The secret meeting convened at eight o'clock in the evening and lasted until two o'clock in the morning. In that time funding and strategies were discussed. The entire group was advised to keep the meeting's business confidential.

The next morning, everyone who had attended the "secret" meeting showed up at his business downtown with a red nose and forehead. Harris had forgotten to turn off the sunlamps and all exposed skin was burned a bright red.

Sparks, who won the election, said, "It felt like God had marked everyone of us at that meeting."

Tom Sparks was a St. Joseph City Commissioner from 1948-1963. He served as mayor from 1955-1962, and remains active in community politics today.

How Senator Humphrey Lost his Seat in St. Joseph

On February 13, 1959, Minnesota Senator Hubert Humphrey was visiting the Twin Cities on a speaking tour. According to the local newspaper, Humphrey was the chairman of a powerful Senate committee, "but he lost a chair to a young Republican of St. Joseph."

Nine-year-old Stephen Hoffmann, the son of Sally and Edward Hoffmann, was waiting with his father in the barber shop of the Whitcomb Hotel when Humphrey stormed into the shop some forty minutes late for an appointment with Hugo Schoenfeld. Schoenfeld had another client in his chair and could not take the senator.

Humphrey saw that Art Chartrand's chair was empty and presumed that he would cut his hair. But Humphrey's appointment had been for 3:20 p.m. It was now a few minutes after four o'clock, and Chartrand informed the tardy senator that the Hoffmanns had this time scheduled every week.

"I'm Hubert Humphrey," the senator announced.

"I'm sorry sir," Chartrand replied. "This young man is next in line. You'll have to wait your turn." Stephen had gotten out of his seat and was heading for the barber chair when the senator arrived. While the men debated, young Hoffman stood between them and watched silently, his head turning from side to side in an effort to follow the dialogue of the two stubborn men.

The senator lost that debate and his seat in the barber chair. As he stomped out of the shop, unshorn, the senator was already rationalizing the incident. He was heard to remark, "I guess I don't really need a haircut."

*This story was submitted by **Sally and Edward Hoffmann** who reside in St. Joseph. Stephen is grown and living in Indiana.*

Stephen Hoffmann
age 9

Stick 'Em Up

On a June morning in 1959, William Mihalik walked into the Whitcomb Hotel coffee shop and noticed a group of people standing around a man dressed in western clothes and wearing a large Mexican sombrero.

Mihalik's stares attracted the cowboy's attention. He drew a six-shooter from his holster, pointed it at Mihalik and said, "What are you looking at?"

In turn, Mihalik drew his police service revolver, pointed it at the cowboy and said, "I've got something for you, too."

Not knowing that Mihalik was a police officer in plain clothes, the cowboy held up his hands and said, "Take it easy. I'm only kidding."

The men introduced themselves and Mihalik learned he had exchanged gun points with Hollywood star Leo Carrillo, better known in the 1950s as "Pancho."

William Mihalik served as the St. Joseph police chief from 1977 to 1982. He worked in law enforcement for 37 years.

This photo shows Mihalik cracking a case in 1968.

How to Get Started in Business

Pasquale and Marianna "Anna" Santaniello were born in Italy before immigrating to Chicago Heights, Illinois. They were married there in 1962. About that time, Anna had an uncle living on the beach in Stevensville who they often visited. One weekend they saw a man being chased on the beach by another man with obviously unfriendly intentions.

Pasquale and his brother, Fred, ran to help the man being chased. He turned out to be Edwardo Veracchi, then owner of the Glenlord Vista Resort. After a successful rescue, the men became instant friends. One thing led to another. The resort was up for sale...the Santaniellos wanted to move to the area...and a deal was struck.

The business was purchased by the two Santaniello brothers who were married to two sisters, Anna and Teresa, along with their brother and two other sisters. Keeping it all in the family didn't work, and after a few years it became obvious that there was not enough income in the resort for four families. Anna and Pasquale became the sole owners in the late 1960s of what has become Santaniello's Glenlord Restaurant and Pizzeria.

The business today seats 110 in the main restaurant, with a summer deck seating an additional 40. In 1990 a 7,000 sq. ft. banquet hall was added.

They originally purchased six cabins and a white frame house with a public dining room. The dining room had a separate entrance from the main part of the house where the Santaniellos lived with their two daughters, Santina and Nadia.

69

There was no heat, no air conditioning and no public restrooms. The cabins also were without heat, air or telephones. The first menu was handwritten by Pasquale and posted in the dining room. Dinner prices were in the range of $3.75.

"Those years were the three hardest years of our lives," says Anna who ran the restaurant while Pasquale worked at Bendix and at Memorial Hospital. "To entice business, we would open when everyone else was closed. We were open on Easter and on Mondays. Once people tried the good food, they came back, but we had to get them in here."

Pasquale ran the restaurant on weekends while Anna tended to the family. He recalls, "One booth in the front was really drafty. No one wanted it, so the last customer would get it."

He remembers one evening when the electricity was out in the dining room. He had to string a wire from a cabin and bring a lamp from the house in order to see to make pizza.

Another time it was raining so hard that people had to move their plates to avoid drips from the roof. In winter it was so cold in the building that people ate wearing their coats. And customers frequently came into the kitchen to help with the dishes just because it was a friendly place to be.

There was a time they had no money for supplies. One brother gave them five pounds of cheese, and a brother-in-law gave them sausage and flour so they could open their doors for another week.

People asked them why they struggled with the resort when Pasquale made good money at Bendix and at the hospital. To Anna the answer was simple. She wanted people to know how good her food was.

"It was a sense of pride. You start with something and you want to finish it," she said with determination. Then she laughed at the memory of those days. "When I think back, I wonder 'How did we do it?' The dining room had a separate entrance from the house and I had to run between the restaurant and the children. It was hard, but we believed in ourselves and we wanted to make it work."

In 1971 Anna was pregnant with their third child, Raffaele. She went into labor on a Friday night and called Pasquale who was working a second shift at Bendix. Then she called her mother—who was 65 years old at the time and didn't speak a word of English—to mind the children and run the restaurant.

On a normal Friday night in those days, the Santaniellos made three or four pizzas. That particular evening, their orders doubled. When Pasquale came flying in from Bendix, he was told to finish the pizzas Anna had started making. With the telephone ringing for more orders and Anna's labor pains increasing, Pasquale put seven pizzas into the oven without cheese. He then whisked Anna away to the hospital, missing a turn on the way even though he worked part-time at Memorial and—in calmer circumstances—could have made the drive blindfolded.

Mama Mia! It's all a part of doing business.

Don't Sweat the Small Stuff
(and remember, it's all small stuff)

Hort Neidlinger was fire chief in St. Joseph from 1962 to 1972. One day a friend of his called the Fire Department on the non-emergency telephone and asked to speak to Hort.

When Hort came to the telephone and he and the friend had exchanged greetings, the man asked Hort if he remembered the place that he had recently purchased.

Hort replied that he remembered the place.

The friend said, "Well, the damn thing is on fire."

Neidlinger often told this story of the man's casual attitude under pressure, and current chief of police, Ted Fleisher, passed it on to us.

St. Joseph City Hall and Fire Station

Harry Horton Neidlinger died in 1990. In addition to serving as chief from 1962-1972, he was captain from 1937 to 1962, and began service as a fireman in 1929.

Hort Neidlinger's Tombstone

Bob Ketelhut, superintendent of the St. Joseph cemeteries, tells about a standing joke between himself and Hort Neidlinger that started when Hort bought a marker. For years, Hort would ask Bob if he was keeping his marker washed. Bob would reply that he was and that he was going to put a fireplug by Hort's marker. Hort asked him not to do that because he didn't want all of the neighborhood dogs stopping by to use the fireplug.

Robert A. Ketelhut has worked in the cemeteries of the city of St. Joseph for 40 years, 19 of those as superintendent of cemeteries. His father, Richard G. Ketelhut, was superintendent of cemeteries before him and worked for the city for 45 years.

I'm Pat Moody

During Pat Moody's early years with WSJM/WIRX radio, circa 1975, he was instructed to finish every news report by identifying himself with the phrase, "I'm Pat Moody."

For one of his programs, Pat conducted a survey of service stations; in that context he visited the Sunoco Station located where Fannie May Candies is now at 2909 Niles Avenue in St. Joseph. An attendant was outside in the driveway and Moody introduced himself saying, "I'm Pat Moody from WSJM/WIRX radio."

The attendant perked up and excitedly said, "Who?"

"Pat Moody from WSJM/WIRX."

Without further explanation, the attendant grabbed Moody by the arm and led him inside saying, "Follow me." As they entered the garage, the attendant shouted to a mechanic who was working under a car, "Hey, Bud. Who are you?"

The mechanic rolled out from under the car, puffed up his chest and mimicked, "I'm Pat Moody," in a resonant voice.

The attendant grinned and pointed at Pat. "Bud, *this is Pat Moody.*"

It was an embarrassing moment for the mechanic who was caught in the act. But they all laughed, and Pat remembers getting lots of help with his survey. After all, isn't imitation the sincerest form of flattery?

Patrick M. Moody *is a celebrity in the twin cities through his work in community service and on his morning radio program called "Moody in the Morning" WSJM-AM.*

The Improvement of Downtown St. Joseph

Note: *Following is an excerpt from George S. Keller's memoirs,* View from the Top.

An opportunity came in the late 1970s to be of some service to the city of St. Joseph, and that experience was as satisfying as any I had in court. My wife Rachel had been instrumental in the mid-1970s in stimulating the city commission to install artificial flowers on the light poles downtown.

We owned real estate there and it was natural for her to seek to beautify the property. There were rumors of a big indoor mall coming to Benton Township and it was uneasily speculated that such a development could herald the demise of St. Joseph in the same manner the Fairplain Plaza had triggered the collapse of downtown Benton Harbor.

"Project Foresight" was launched to implement a downtown revitalization in St. Joseph to avoid Benton Harbor's fate. Ultimately, a Downtown Development Authority (DDA) was created under a legislative enactment and I was made the first chairman. This was a position largely earned through Rachel's efforts to bring beauty to the downtown which already showed signs of deterioration.

That early DDA had distinguished personnel on it including Jack Sparks, John Fetters, Richard Schanze, Ray Carlson, Theodore Bestervelt, LeRoy Hornack and Clifford Emlong. Ronald Momany brought enthusiasm and guidance to his post of DDA executive director. William Sinclair, newly appointed city manager, joined in energetically to advance the DDA goals of reviving the central business district. Whirlpool Corporation, always a staunch supporter of anything beneficial to the area, loaned employee Len Hardke to act as the professional planner of the project.

Uniquely, no funding was sought from federal or state sources. We were determined to be free of governmental control and to make this an entirely local endeavor.

More than $800,000 was raised through contributions from civic-minded individuals and corporations. The business district properties were assessed a special tax. John Stubblefield, president of Peoples State Bank and the St. Joseph Improvement Association, was a tower of strength and inspiration. He contributed money to purchase the Colonel Wallace home on the southeast corner of State and Elm Streets, along with property across the street, to construct critically needed parking lots.

The demolition of the Wallace house was angrily disapproved by many activists who claimed the house was an historical landmark. At a heated meeting of the city commission, my proposal that a parking lot was the best use for the property triggered angry denunciation of Stubblefield and myself. We were figuratively hung in effigy. Heated meetings ensued between proponents of revitalization and those who favored maintenance of the status quo.

When we started ripping up State Street to make it one-way with amenities of trees, decorative lighting, benches and flower pots there were some who complained that we were destroying the community. But St. Joseph was coming back to life.

It was more than the central business core that benefited; it was the entire community which began to recognize the worth of the improvement project. DDA doctrine expressed that if the heart of the city was transformed into a pleasant place to shop and do business, St. Joseph's unique location on Lake Michigan would provide the attraction to make the city an exciting center for people miles around to enjoy.

We then formed a new chamber of commerce to represent the business and professional people in St. Joseph. That organization became St. Joseph Today with its own board of directors and an executive director (initally Len Hardke, then Patti Sizer, and her successor, Kathy Zerler). St. Joseph Today was destined to plan events and festivals to attract shoppers to the city.

The plan worked. The magnificent Krasl Art Center, a gift of George and Olga Krasl, was to rise on Lake Boulevard. The Maud Preston Palenske Memorial Library and gardens would be enlarged and beautified. The John E.N. Howard Bandshell with its concerts and the many festivals promoted by St. Joseph Today were all to have their input in creating a city with the ambiance, vitality and interest to encourage merchants, professionals and various business interests to be proudly identified with the downtown.

Visiting officials from communities near and far came to St. Joseph to see what had been accomplished with local talent and resources, without help or interference from federal and state governments.

The Orchards Mall was no longer a threat to the business interests in St. Joseph. We held our own proudly. St.

Joseph became a classic prototype of what a small town can do to renew its vitality. The logo formulated by Don Johnson for St. Joseph Today remains symbolic of that renewed vitality, enthusiasm and ambiance of a community which graciously says to one and all: "Come, enjoy what we have here."

George S. Keller is an attorney who has lived in St. Joseph since 1965.

Note: *Read* On the Banks of the Ole St. Joe *for more information on the development of downtown St. Joseph.*

George and Rachel Keller

Saluting St. Joseph's
Decade of Development
1979-1989

Following are the winning poem and song from a contest held as part of the city-wide celebration commemorating ten years of renovations in downtown St. Joseph.

<u>First Place Poem</u>

St. Joe Today
by Dawn Consolino, Coloma

St. Joe Today
Is such a lovely sight;
There's ample parking
And store fronts bright.

St. Joe Today
Is a sparkling town;
Whether on the beach
Or right downtown.

The events and festivals
Bring us lots of trade;
We can shop downtown
Or enjoy a parade.

St. Joe Today
Is a city on the bluff.
Always building and growing,
I just can't say enough.

St. Joe Today
by Nicholas G. Auringer, St. Joseph

Back in the days when our country was young
Our forefathers trodded across the land,
In search of a site to build a new life
And settled right here where I stand.

St. Joe Today, keep growing in your way
I'm proud of everything you have become,
St. Joe. Today, it's here I'm going to stay
I'll bask in the warmth of your sun.
We are as one.

And from the beginning, your faith hasn't changed
Its people are why you have grown.
There is a beginning for each of your dreams
Come share in a dream all your own.

St. Joe Today, keep growing in your way
I'm proud of everything you have become,
St. Joe. Today, it's here I'm going to stay
I'll bask in the warmth of your sun.
We are as one.

EXPERIENCE
ST. joseph TOdAY

Censorship at the Whitcomb

In 1981, Whitcomb Tower's activities director, Rosemary Ritter, started a newspaper reading group for the facility's visually handicapped residents. It was an immediate success and approximately 17 seniors regularly attended the afternoon sessions (which continue today with volunteer readers). Ritter read national and local news highlights from the *Herald-Palladium* as well as sports, feature stories, the weather, obituaries and other items of interest to the listeners.

One column the residents always wanted to hear was by Ann Landers. On one occasion Ritter felt that one of the letters to Landers was too sexually explicit for the refined ears of her listeners, so she simply overlooked it and went on to another article.

She was interrupted by Edith Hillberg, a totally blind resident, who asked if there was only one letter in Lander's column that day.

Ritter replied, "No, but I cannot read the other."

Hillberg was obviously perturbed. She demanded to know why the other letter could not be read.

Ritter said it was just too sexy.

"Well," Hillberg said, "and who are you to censor what we hear? We have all lived a lot longer than you have and there is nothing we haven't already seen or heard. So please read the column."

Rosemary Ritter was born in St. Joseph and has lived here most of her life. During her career at the Whitcomb she advanced from activities director to director of public relations and marketing.

Flip's Donut Shop

Many residents remember Flip's Donut Shop which was open all night while Flip made doughnuts for the next morning. The scent of frying batter, the delicious taste of warm doughnuts and the camaraderie of gathering at 607 Broad Street in the wee hours of the morning made Flip's a special place.

Business at Flip's was conducted on the honor system; that is, customers made their own change from his cash register. The walls of Flip's small shop were covered with old photographs, quotable and not so notable quotes, trophies, antiques and local memorabilia.

Rob Orlaske became an addition to the wall—much to his embarrassment—after a 3:30 a.m. visit to Flip's in the early 1980s. Flip snapped a photograph of him studying a *Penthouse* centerfold of former Miss America, Vanessa Williams, who was relieved of her title as a result of the magazine's feature story. Rob said he was only reading the story!

Robert C. Orlaske is a partner in Century 21 Orlaske-Dillingham real estate services. He has lived in St. Joseph all his life.

Neighbors
by Dottie Ruggles Gietler

Now neighbors in the neighborhood are really cool.
Some do stuff like run the school.
Some are teachers; some are cooks.
Some keep track of library books.
Some sweep floors; some call your dad.
And some take care of you when you're bad.

Chorus:
We are neighbors and that's real good.
We live right here in the neighborhood.
Your neighborhood is really fine.
It's next to his and next to mine.

Now down the street from where I live
Is a place that's got a lot to give.
You can swim and jog, play basketball.
This family center has got it all.
You can exercise or learn to dive,
Lift weights, karate and that's no jive.
You better listen to what I say;
This place is called the YMCA.

Chorus...

In my neighborhood's a real great place.
You can learn to draw pictures of a person's face.
You can paint and sculpt, do decoupage.
They even make art out of old garbage.
Now I'm not giving you a razzle dazzle.
The place I'm talkin' 'bout is called the Krasl.

Chorus...

Down the street from me are some real neat stores.
They even have old wooden floors.
You can buy most anything your heart desires
From books and puzzles to rubber tires.
Excuse me, please; I've got to go.
I do my shopping in ole St. Joe.

Chorus...

When I get sick, I'll be all right
Whether it's morning or in the night.
There's some folks that work around the clock
In the hospital that's in my block.
They treat you right, feed you real good food.
They even read you stories if you're in the mood.
When I think of doing a job that size,
I wish I could give them all a prize.

Chorus...

This rap song was written in 1985 by **Dottie Ruggles Gietler** *during a study of neighborhoods by her Lincoln Elementary School second graders. Gietler has lived in the area all her life and is a teacher in the St. Joseph Public Schools.*

Top row, left to right: *Anthony Belski, Dottie Gietler, Jason Muscoe, Andrea Auringer, Matthew Farmer, Lori Nye, Chris Mustell, Emily Adams. Second row: Anu Sarda, Michael Kutz, Maggie McGrath, Michael Finch. Third row: James Estkowski, Kristy Janke, Jeff Bell, Michelle Wyngarden, Sara Seltmann, Robert Burdine, Fritz Harmon, Melissa Thomas. Bottom row: Eric Brant, Chrisy Craft, Chris Robertson, Krissy Shuck, Melissa Hopp, Paul Mandigo.*

St. Joseph's First Bed & Breakfast

In July of 1987, the South Cliff Inn, St. Joseph's first bed and breakfast at 1900 Lakeshore Drive, was ready for a coat of interior paint after extensive remodeling by the present innkeeper Bill Swisher and his former partners.

Swisher had carefully chosen the paint, ordered the primer tinted to match, picked up 20 gallons of the stuff from a local paint store, taped and covered everything in the three-story house that was not to be painted and left for the weekend. He had been working intensely on the house and needed a break. His partners were slated to spray paint the entire interior in his absence.

When Swisher returned the following Monday, a knot began to form in his stomach. The house did not appear as bright through the windows as he had imagined it would be with the light color of paint he had selected. The knot grew when he walked through the door. The entire interior was a coffee-colored brown instead of the near white color he had chosen.

The Labor Day deadline raced through his mind. He had guests booked for that weekend and not only did he have a brown house to put them in—there was a lot of additional renovation work yet to be finished.

Trying to keep his rage under control, Swisher contacted his partners who said they thought the dark paint was a tad radical but had agreed to leave all of the creative decisions up to him. They assumed he had changed his mind about the off-white paint. He then called the paint store manager who apologized profusely for the mistake and agreed to mix the correct paint at no charge.

But things were not as simple as they seemed. In addition to the hassle with paint, Swisher had had a weekend of problems with his car keys. First, he left his car in a friend's driveway in Grand Rapids while they headed for Traverse City in another vehicle. When he returned to Grand Rapids with his car keys still in Traverse City, he borrowed the friend's car with the promise of a swift return of the car and his spare keys. No problem, yet.

But the brown paint caused his usual good sense to slip away. When he found himself on the return trip to Grand Rapids still without his keys, his grip on reality became a thing of the past. Chiding himself for his forgetfulness, Swisher drove back to St. Joseph, got the keys, returned the friend's car, retrieved his own and arrived at the South Cliff Inn with a brown cloud surrounding his temperament.

He made a rational decision to wait a few days before confronting the hapless paint store manager. When he did, he inadvertently locked the keys in the ignition. Still cool at this point, Swisher arranged to have a local car dealer make a replacement key for his vehicle. (His own spare set was still in Traverse City.)

The dealer's key arrived—hours later—and didn't fit. With time slipping by and the pressure of the Labor Day deadline foremost in his consciousness, Swisher made the only just decision under the circumstances. He calmly entered the paint store, borrowed a hammer and smashed the passenger window in his car. With the store employees gaping in the doorway, he loaded 20 cans of paint into the car and drove away. He said he truly felt better after that.

William E. Swisher still runs the South Cliff Inn which underwent a second renovation in 1990. Whenever anger crops up, Bill finds that a simple piece of glass and a hammer provide a sure cure.

South Cliff Inn

Maestro John E.N. Howard

When John Howard retired from St. Joseph's Municipal Band on Labor Day in 1987, he said, "I want to walk away before they have to carry me off." He smiled boyishly, his face belying his 68 years. "I'd love to sit in the reed section and play the sax or the clarinet," he added.

1987 marked Howard's 40th year as music director and maestro for St. Joseph's municipal musicians. He stepped away from the podium, but not from the city. Now, he is often seen enjoying retirement the way it's supposed to be. With his beautiful wife Dede at his side, Howard frequents a downtown coffee shop, shops locally and supports area cultural events. In 1990 he appeared as the guest conductor when the United States Coast Guard Band performed in the bandshell named after him.

Born in Oklahoma City on July 8, 1919, Howard was the youngest of four children in the family of R.C. and Hettie Howard. He graduated from high school in Oklahoma City before moving on to Ann Arbor and the University of Michigan.

Howard first became involved in music in elementary school when he was given a saxophone by a relative. He learned how to play it by studying books. In junior high, he was a member of the school band and played sax and percussion. In high school, he expanded to playing flute, bassoon, clarinet and cello.

While in Ann Arbor, he worked his way through two degrees in music by playing in a dance band. He primarily played saxophone and clarinet for clubs, fraternity houses, the Michigan Union and the Michigan League.

During class hours, instruction in all instruments was required. "We had to know a little about all instruments, not so we could perform with them all, but so we could teach the basics of each one," he said of his graduate and undergraduate work. After 39 months in the United States Army Signal Corps, the Army Air Corps, Infantry and Artillery groups, Howard returned to the University of Michigan to work on a doctorate in music.

He married Lillian VanderHeuvel in September, 1942. They had two sons, Steven and Brian. Lillian passed away in December, 1981. Steven died in May, 1983. Howard married the former Dede Edinger in December, 1983.

A former music teacher, Howard began directing St. Joseph's Municipal Band in 1948. He favored the marches of John Phillips Sousa, but always arranged the Sunday and holiday concerts with a range of musical tastes in mind. A typical program might have included selections from Claude T. Smith, Peter Tschaikowsky, Duke Ellington and Johnny Mercer as well as Sousa.

The audiences who crowded the Lake Bluff Park bandshell were varied, too. From boaters idling in the river below, to residents and guests of the nearby Whitcomb Tower, Lakeview Terrace and Holiday Inn who listened from their balconies and open windows, to the parents, children and friends who gathered on the benches, bleachers and lawns, the summer municipal band concerts comprised what one writer dubbed "some of the best outdoor music in America."

There are few adjectives to describe what Howard has given to the community. The open concrete bandshell designed by Wayne Hatfield and Associates is placed with a view of the St. Joseph River, Lake Michigan and the North Pier lighthouse. Fresh breezes fan the audience as the sun sets during the evening performances. It doesn't get much better, and to top it off, the music is superlative.

About 55 musicians gather weekly in the bandshell during the summer to play light classics, soothing ballads and rousing marches. The performances have been going on in St. Joseph for more than 60 years, and the band is one of few that is still municipally sponsored.

The John E.N. Howard Bandshell is located on the corner of Lake Boulevard and Port Street in Lake Bluff Park just west of Business Loop I-94 (Main Street) in downtown St. Joseph. Stop by and stay a while. Concerts are held from the last Sunday in June to Labor Day at 3:30 & 7:30 p.m. on Sundays and holidays.

Creative Brochures

In 1990 and 1991 Barb Durflinger's third graders at E.P. Clarke School in St. Joseph created travel brochures for our great city. Here's what some of the eight and nine-year-old students wrote inside their colorful brochures:

Welcome to St. Joseph, Michigan.
We hope you enjoy your visit here.
You'll love the sunsets.
I think you'll like the beach, too.

Saint Joe is a nice place.

St. Joe is rad!

I love St. Joe!
You'll love the lake.

St. Joe has lots of good fruit to eat and
lots of space to grow.
And you can tell your neighbor it is the right place to go.

Enjoy the beauty of the lake.
It is a wonderful fishing place.
Also nice for a picnic.
And a great boating place.
The birds are a lovely sight.

Spend a day at the beautiful lake.
Watch the sunrise and the sunset.

The bluff is beautiful.
St. Joseph has a very pretty lake with a pier on it.
St. Joe has many parks that are very fun.

Fruit markets are a perfect place
to buy fruit in the summer.

Fishing in summer is fun.

These brochures are distributed by St. Joseph Today in
very special "Welcome Packets" that go to people who are
considering moving to our area. We received about 30
handmade brochures each year and could use hundreds
more. We wish to sincerely thank Mrs. Durflinger for
promoting our area by instilling an appreciation for the
community in her students.

*Barbara C. Durflinger has lived in St. Joseph 19 years. She has
been a teacher with the St. Joseph Public Schools for eight years.*

*Back row, left to right: Jenny Willming (kneeling), Tracy Sjoberg,
Cara Tarantino, Andy Gustafson, Richard Evans, Alex Polnaszek,
Dawn Wesner, Jill Shafer (kneeling). Middle row, left to right:
Elizabeth Westerhof, Stephanie Miller, Sarah Mundy, Josh King,
Adam Barrett, Alina Fry. Front row, left to right: Emma Senecal,
Jeff Tichenor, Shaun Tvetmarken, Brad Shushman, Erin Gohlke,
Linda Viengmyxay, Carolyn Stevens.*

95

Santa Gets Caught with his Pants Down

When Emil Tosi owned Tosi's Restaurant, he began a tradition of inviting underprivileged children to lunch with Santa Claus. Tosi carried on this practice for approximately 20 years, but it was discontinued by subsequent owners.

When Marge and Arnie Wiatrowski and Gary Manigold became partners with Ginger and Charles Mostov in the late 1980s, they decided to revive the tradition. Marge and company worked with the Salvation Army and the YMCA Uncles to give needy children a special lunch on a Saturday in December.

Things went without a hitch for the first two years of this joint project. Tosi's provided the food and fruit baskets for the children, and the Salvation Army contributed another gift for each of the approximately 75 children who were invited to attend.

It appeared that things were going smoothly during the 1990 luncheon when Santa attempted to make his retreat and—without provocation—his pants fell down around his ankles. Imagine the embarrassment of Santa (aka Arnie Wiatrowski) as the children stared in disbelief and YMCA Uncles' leader, Rev. Charles Frandsen, said, "Santa, you lost your pants!"

Emil Tosi founded Tosi's Restaurant in 1939 in Stevensville.

High Goals

Marilyn Peterson recalls an evening in 1990 when her daughter Monica, a senior at St. Joseph High School, returned home from her part-time job at the Peoples State Bank. She had been working there for several months and had been observing the different departments in the bank as well as the many types of jobs.

Monica told her mother she had decided on the job she would like to have at the bank. "I want Mr. Schanze's job," the teenager said.

Marilyn Peterson has lived in the southwestern Michigan area all her life. She is married to Judge David M. Peterson and they are raising their two children in St. Joseph. Richard Schanze is the chief operating officer at the Peoples State Bank.

Richard Schanze

Wilbur's Ice Cream

One of the legends of St. Joseph is about ice cream—
Wilbur's ice cream.

In summer, people walking with waffle cones in hand are
a familiar sight in the vicinity of the little shop at 609
Broad Street. With faces fixed in tranquil gazes, paces
slow to licking speed.

Homemade from cream, milk, eggs and sugar, ice cream is
a natural treat. All ice cream begins with those four
simple ingredients. It's how they are mixed together that
makes the difference.

*Customers and staff of Wilbur's Ice Cream at 609 Broad
Street in downtown St. Joseph circa 1926.*

At Wilbur's the recipe is a secret that has been handed down from the shop's original owners, George and Nellie Wilbur, who started business in downtown St. Joseph in 1926. At that time, the Wilburs served nine flavors of ice cream.

Today, more than 52 flavors are produced in a tiny kitchen. Current owners Delores "Dee" and Stephen Reagan still won't divulge the secret ingredients of their ice cream.

As the youngest of 12 children in a farm family, Dee learned early about cooking with fresh ingredients. She also learned to experiment. She says, "With ice cream, if you stick with it and experiment, it will turn out okay. Of course, you have to start with good basic ingredients." Just like the old days.

The red, white and blue interior has nothing to do with the fact that Steve is a third cousin of former president Ronald Reagan. But there is a framed red, white and blue photograph of the president and first lady Nancy Reagan hanging prominently on the east wall of the shop.

On the Fourth of July in Wilbur's you can get red, white and blue ice cream made with vanilla, red raspberries and blueberries. It's called Fireworks!

Dee makes German chocolate cake from scratch for her ice cream confection of the same name. Homemade toffee goes into her English Toffee ice cream, and egg custard is specially prepared for the flavor called Egg Nog. Fresh brownies, almond pralines and seasonal Michigan fruits are also used.

A house specialty is Oreo Cookie ice cream. Dee Reagan makes and serves an average of 40 gallons of it every week and still sells out regularly. An estimated 400 people buy ice cream from Wilbur's Ice Cream and Sandwich Shoppe every day during summer. On Sundays and holidays, with the St. Joseph Municipal Band Concerts nearby, the numbers are even greater.

Other unusual flavors from Dee Reagan's kitchen include Peach Yogurt, Chocolate Silk, and E.T. made with Reese's Pieces. Butter pecan and strawberry are two of the most popular flavors. "But the old folks still like vanilla," says Steve Reagan. "There are no nuts in it to get caught in their teeth."

"It is impossible to live pleasurably without living prudently, and honorably, and justly; or to live prudently, and honorably, and justly, without living pleasurably."

Epicurus

W. Playing

A Daring Bike Ride

The year was 1900. Dorothy Davis (later Brightup) and her friend Mabel (later Zick) were riding their bicycles in Lake Bluff Park. One thing led to another and the two sixteen-year-old girls dared each other to ride down the bluff. Dorothy did it.

Years later she would tell this story to her granddaughter, Sharon Brightup Anstey, and confess, "My dear, that was the scariest ride I *ever* had, but I didn't fall...all the way to Silver Beach!"

Dorothy Davis Brightup was the daughter of Byron and Elizabeth Davis of Stevensville. She later became Mrs. Albert Brightup of St. Joseph and Benton Harbor. Sharon Anstey lives in Benton Harbor and never visits Lake Bluff Park without thinking of and trying to picture her grandmother riding down the hill on her bike.

The Night the School Bell Rang

Marion S. McKenna remembers her father, Stanley A. Stock, telling of the night he and several friends took clothesline from their homes, tied them together, climbed up the fire escape and attached one end to the bell in the former Washington School (now KitchenAid) bell tower at 701 Main Street.

They rang the bell late one night circa 1908 causing the neighborhood to wake up and wonder what was happening. McKenna does not recall the consequences of this prank, if there were any. She remembers her father telling the story with obvious enjoyment at "pulling one over" on the neighborhood.

Washington School/KitchenAid

Marion McKenna has lived in the area all of her life. At the time of this story, her father resided at 1408 Forres Avenue in St. Joseph. He became an associate with his father, Max, in the M.W. Stock and Sons Construction Company.

House of David Baseball Memories

Poetic Justice...

In the 1920s and 1930s, when the House of David team was traveling all over the nation, Dave Harris played third base. Player and team manager Tom Dewhirst recalls a game in the Mouse River Park, west of Minot, North Dakota, where a fellow in the bleachers razzed Harris continually about his playing and his long hair.

In that park the wooden bleachers ran all around the playing field and this fellow sat near the third base line. After a few innings of verbal abuse, Harris came up to bat amid more jeers from this loudmouthed fan. Spectators and players divided their attention between Harris at bat and the screaming fan in the bleachers. A pitch was thrown and Harris connected.

Harris' ball soared directly into the vocal fan. People in the crowd wondered whether it was great skill or simple inadvertency. In any case, the action stopped the fellow's razzing and left him apologizing for the balance of the game.

Pluto Water...

After World War I glass bottles were scarce and House of David members would gather up all of the bottles they could find, sterilize them and fill them with soda to sell at the baseball games. The bottles might be filled with strawberry soda or lemon water and this was marked on the cap, but the bottle itself was likely to be embossed with something entirely different. (In addition to making their own soda, members also made sugar cones, ice cream from ice chopped out of the Paw Paw River, roasted peanuts, popped corn and candy.)

Dewhirst remembers a woman in the stands on a particularly hot day who wanted a soda and told him she'd take anything he had so long as it was wet and cold. The lemon water she received, however, was in a bottle embossed with "Pluto Water" and she exclaimed, "Lausy me, I don't want Pluto Water!" Pluto Water was a laxative manufactured in French Lick, Indiana.

Long Hair and Beards...
In the early 1900s, all House of David baseball club players were members of the religious colony. One of the House of David requirements is that their members do not cut their hair. As the team began traveling and the competition grew a little stiffer, House of David team managers recruited players from outside the sect to supplement the roster and maintain their outstanding reputation. The players who were hired for the team were required to wear the House of David uniform as well as long hair and a beard.

Dewhirst remembers that this worked for the team in more ways than one. In the 1920s and 1930s publicity was adequate, but like the team, it needed reinforcement. After the members checked into hotels, they would walk down the main streets of the towns where games were scheduled. Few people in those days wore long hair and beards, so their presence alone attracted attention and one person after another was seen coming out of shops to stand on the sidewalk and stare. It was good advertising for the games, and Dewhirst presumes that the telephones inside the stores were ringing with news of the bearded players.

Another time, the manager of a team in Tacoma, Washington walked over to the House of David bench and asked if the members would be insulted if his team came out wearing long beards. Dewhirst said they would not be offended.

The next inning, the opposing team came out wearing beards down to their waist lines. The House of David beards looked skimpy in comparison.

One player got caught between first and second base. As he ran back and forth his long beard went one way and then the other. House of David players laughed so hard they let him get safely to second base.

The Traveling Team...
The House of David used the first portable lighting system with the traveling team. Prior to lights on the field, games were played in the afternoon or early evening when they were called "Twilight Games."

With lights, the team sometimes played three games a day. They would play in the morning in one town, travel forty or fifty miles and play a doubleheader later in the day.

In those days there were no paved roads and signage was poor or nonexistent. Dewhirst recalls that it was very common to have to open a gate along the main road, pass through it and then close it behind the cars.

Tires also were very poor then and the traveling team caravan carried several sets of tires to be assured of getting from one town to the next.

The team trained in Hot Springs, Arkansas and Mineral Wells, Texas as well as other locations in the south. They played the minor league teams, and sometimes played against major league clubs during spring training or in exhibition games. The House of David team traveled throughout the United States and Canada, and took along one member who did nothing but distribute literature and sell postcards.

H. Thomas Dewhirst was a player and manager of the House of David Baseball Club from 1929-1937.

And He Turned Out So Well

Ed Conrad laughs when he remembers the times Benton Harbor policeman Ezra Lewis pulled him over for having straight pipes instead of a muffler installed on his 1933 Ford. "My buddies and I would drag race right through Main Street in downtown Benton Harbor. We all had straight pipes on our cars so we sounded like a fleet of motor boats. We would race with the engines wide open. Officer Lewis took us into the station at least five times and made us replace our mufflers. He would tell us each time that the next time it happened he would impound our cars."

Ed's '33 Ford

Edward J. Conrad is the executive vice president of the Twin Cities Area Chamber of Commerce and a former officer of the NBD F & M Bank.

The Saga of Dr. Clell K. Johnson
or
A Community Christmas Disaster

In 1934, during the height of the Great Depression, Dr. Clell "Doc" Johnson opened a dental office in St. Joseph's 505 (Pleasant Street) Building. He was unacquainted with anyone in the town, but had driven through St. Joseph on his way to Chicago a few years prior and decided that this was where he wanted to practice when he finished dental school.

He had a room at the Lakeview Hotel across the street from the Whitcomb. The night before New Year's Eve, he came back from his office and the night clerk informed him that Mary Walker, owner of the Lakeview, was having a party for her lady friends and wanted him to join them and be their bartender. He was delighted to oblige and spent the evening visiting and sampling the brew.

It was a blizzardy night and when Mrs. Carroll of Benton Harbor tried to leave the party her car wouldn't start. Johnson's Model A Ford was parked right behind her car so he gave her a gentle push and then swung around the corner of Ship and State Street.

All of a sudden he found himself trying to get out from under the community Christmas tree which stood in the middle of the State and Pleasant Street intersection. He had unwittingly driven through it and carried it up to Lucker's Butcher shop at 310 State Street. (This was later declared a "record" after several more drivers knocked the tree down in subsequent years.)

Johnson tried to back up but his transmission had failed. Just then an unknown man came by and said, "Doc, I have a chain and I'll pull your car over to the garage at the Dennis Hotel and no one will be the wiser."

However, another bystander headed directly to McCracken's Bar & Grill and told everyone there that someone with such and such a license number had knocked down the Christmas tree. Policemen Carl Schuett and Ollie Slater were in the grill and said, "That's Doc Johnson." The policemen went to the hotel and helped the night clerk put Johnson to bed.

Mary Walker felt badly about the incident and tried to keep it out of the newspaper. But Rex Wynkoop, then editor of the *Herald-Press,* said the story was too good to let go and gave it a big spread. The story also appeared in the *South Bend Tribune.*

Johnson felt his dental practice would probably be ruined since he had been in town for only four months. Instead the publicity made him a town celebrity and his practice grew.

Edward Brown, city attorney, and Art Mollhagen, city assessor, concocted a fancy bill charging Johnson $35.00 for broken lights. For several years afterward, when the Christmas tree was erected, Johnson received many postcards warning him to watch out for the tree.

A few times through the years, Johnson's friend Willard Banyon, a publisher of the *Herald-Palladium*, placed an item in the "Do You Remember" column saying, "Dr. Clell Johnson knocked down the community Christmas tree on December 30, due to a foggy interior."

AFTER THE FIRST FORTY YEARS OF PRACTICE THE
SECOND SHOULD BE A BREEZE! CONGRATULATIONS —
MAC & ART.

For his 40th birthday, Johnson received a framed cartoon
of the tree accident drawn by Art Poinier, editorial cartoonist for the Detroit News. (In the 1930s, Poinier lived
in St. Joseph and drew a serial cartoon called "Jitter the
Monkey.") Poinier's caption reads, "After the first forty
years of practice the second should be a breeze! Congratulations—Mac & Art."

*This story was submitted by **Virginia Johnson** who married Clell K.
Johnson in 1938. She has lived in the twin cities for 52 years, and has
worked as a teacher, housewife and volunteer. Clell died on February
10, 1990.*

The Optimist...
Virginia also relates an incident that happened one
evening when the Johnsons were sitting on their patio.
The Tom Gillespie family lived next door, and the two
Niles Avenue families were close friends for more than 20
years.

That afternoon, Tom Gillespie had spent considerable
time washing storm windows and stacking them in the
garage. He finished in time to dress for the annual

The Gillespies

Policemen's Ball. As the chief of police in St. Joseph, he was expected to stay until the end of the party.

When Gillespie and his wife Mary returned late that evening, he let her out at the front door and drove into the garage. Immediately, the Johnsons heard a great crash.

Gillespie walked out of the garage with a silly expression on his face and said, "Well, I won't have to put up those damn things this year."

Thomas Gillespie was the St. Joseph Police Chief from 1947 to 1977.

The Johnsons

The Lake View Round Table

In the 1930s the dining room at the Lakeview Hotel, operated by the Lindahls, was a popular place. During lunchtime, young professionals including secretaries, lawyers, teachers and others gathered regularly at a large round table.

The group included Joseph Killian, Edward Brown, Myron Wolcott, Willard Banyon, Dale and Dalton Seymour, Dr. Clell "Doc" Johnson, Nelson Foulkes, Ray Miller, Dick Merson, Art Poinier, Ed Sanborn, Lola McCulloch, Lois Leatherstone, Gladys Goodwin, Alice German, Jean and Louise Stratton, Jim and Ruth Peaslee, and Edward Hoffmann. Others joined the group at times, but these were the regulars and their spouses were included in the social activities. According to Virginia Johnson, when one of them married, moved or had a party for any other reason, their celebrations were extremely festive and noisy.

One memorable evening, as recalled by Johnson, was a birthday party for Willard "Bill" Banyon whose birthday was December 24th. Annually on that afternoon, Banyon's wife, Mary Louise, invited the Lake View Round Table and others to celebrate the occasion and have a bit of Christmas cheer.

In anticipation of this event, Joseph Killian and Doc Johnson arranged to have Louis Kerlikowske deliver eight Irish Setter puppies to Bill's party as his gift. The puppies arrived on board the Kerlikowske hearse (as Kerley was the director of the funeral home now known as Kerley & Starks).

The puppies belonged to Jack and Diane Ryan and were released from their mother with the stipulation that they would be returned early in the evening since they had not been weaned. When the party was over, Bill innocently asked who was designated to return the puppies. He was told that was his problem—but take them soon as they were yelping and it was time to feed them.

Party given by Ed Brown in December, 1938. Left to right. Standing: Dick Merson, Marie Weber. Second row: Lola McCullough, Virginia Johnson, Lois Featherstone, Alice German, Maurice Weber, Joe and Alice Killian (in chair). Front row: Doc Johnson (in chair), Gladys Goodwin, Rex Wynkoop, Ed Brown, Laura Witt. Photo by Ray Miller.

January 12, 1939. Left to right. Back row: Robert Crook, Al Steinel, Nellie Foulkes, Nora Laughlin, Joe Killian, Ed Brown. Middle row: Hale (leaning), Lois Featherstone, Alice German, Lola McCullough, Myron Wolcott, Art Poinier. Front row: Bill Banyon (kneeling), Ruth Westervelt, Dick Merson, Alice Killian, Eddie Sanborn, Virginia Johnson, Lillian Steinel, Gladys Goodwin, Doc Johnson. Photo by Ray Miller.

* * *

On another occasion, circa 1936, the round table challenged the St. Joseph merchants to a baseball game to be played during the merchants picnic at Tabor Farm Resort. These round table members dressed up in long underwear and baseball caps. Score unknown.

Front row, left to right: Howard Ross, Doc Johnson, Mike Boyce, Arthur Poinier. Back row, left to right: Arthur Berk, Carl Schultz, Harry Sahlin, Joseph Killian, Dick Merson, Bob Gillespie, Maurice Weber, Ray Miller. (Photo identification provided by Bob Gillespie.)

Harry Diffenderfer

Known as "Diff" and as "the King of Swing," Harry H. Diffenderfer was a popular band leader in Michigan and Indiana for nearly 61 years. In 1972 at the age of 81, he retired his baton for health reasons but remained active as a limited partner in the stock brokerage firm of William C. Roney & Company.

Born in 1890 in Cambridge City, Indiana, he played the coronet at age nine and went on to attend the Indianapolis School of Business and the Drake School of Music in Chicago. As a teenager, Diffenderfer played with Buckskin Bill's Wild West show in southern Indiana. In 1910, he moved to Knightstown, Indiana and formed his first dance band while working for the Pennsylvania Railroad.

That nine-member group played at the Claypool Hotel during the Indy 500 as well as many other places in Indianapolis. During that period, the band adopted "Honeymoon" from the 1906 musical *The Time, The Place and The Girl* as its theme song.

He referred to his bands as a "hobby" and kept them going when he moved to Benton Harbor in 1934. A *News-Palladium* article by Alan Arend dated Thursday, January 20, 1972, quoted Diffenderfer as saying, "I remember arriving in town on a Sunday night, January 1, and by Thursday I had a band organized and we played that night at the old Higman Park Villa."

Locally, some of his band members were Norma Granzow, Goldie Lockman, John E.N. Howard, E.C. Sodergren, Warren Colby, Gladys Herbertson, John Boyce, Jimmy Miller, Tom Robbins, Paul Bridgham, Southard

Busdicker, Arnold Lesser, Ray Norberg, Bill Glines, Ed Bagatini, Bill Curtin and Stan Ray.

According to the newspaper article, Diffenderfer and his bands played "at nearly every top spot in the area, at country clubs, proms, society club dances, corporation benefits, weddings, etc." They appeared at Ray-Ted's (now Schuler's) in the late 1930s and were the house group for Berrien Hills Country Club for thirty years. They also entertained at the Veteran's Hospital in Battle Creek once a month for two years in 1947-48 with a 100-member choir that Diffenderfer directed. This latter engagement was supported by the federal government which paid $1,000 a month for the performances.

Diffenderfer's style emulated the sounds of Jimmy and Tommy Dorsey and Glenn Miller. He said he liked to play "sweet" music, and many people remember "Diff" as a local symbol of big band music.

Information for this story was supplied by **Thomas and Mary Robbins** *of St. Joseph. Tom played trumpet with "Diff" and other local groups for many years. He is retired from the Whirlpool Corporation.*

*The Harry H. Diffenderfer Band in circa 1967. Front row,
left to right: Perry Francisco, tenor sax; E. C. Sodergren,
alto sax; Stuart Smith, alto sax; Larry Blyly, tenor sax.
Back row: Jim Bittner, trumpet; Tom Robbins, trumpet;
Elmer Taylor, trumpet; Ray Norberg, trombone.
Standing: Diffenderfer; Lynn Davis, drums; Stan Ray,
bass. Seated at piano is Bob Brown.*

A Twin Cities Baseball Story

Not too long after the end of World War II, there were two especially fine baseball teams in the twin cities known as the Benton Harbor Buds and the St. Joe Auscos. Rivalry between the teams was intense and when they played, the games were sellouts.

The Buds home field was in the House of David park off of East Britain and Empire Avenues (later the House of David R.V. & Trailer Park) in Benton Harbor, while the Auscos played at the classy Tiscornia Field in back of the Auto Specialties Plant on what was then an extension of State Street and is now Upton Drive.

One year, Art Morse and Tom Lyons attended a Buds Vs. Auscos match at the House of David field. They sat directly behind St. Joseph's beloved funeral director, Louis Kerlikowske, known to all as "Kerley." Kerley was a rabid baseball fan who rooted for the Auscos while Morse's loyalty was with the Buds. Naturally, a bit of friendly rivalry existed in the stands as well as on the field that day.

During the game there was a very close play at home plate. The umpire called the Ausco player "out." Boos by the Ausco fans shook the old wooden bleachers. Morse and Kerley argued back and forth as to how each of them perceived the play.

Kerley leaned forward, made a megaphone with his hands and laughingly hollered, "Kill the umpire!"

Morse stood up and exclaimed to everyone within earshot, "You heard it folks. Kerley's out drumming up business!"

Tiscornia Field

In the 1940s, after the Benton Harbor Buds disbanded and the House of David cut their baseball program back to a traveling team only, a group of athletes formed a team called the St. Joe Merchants.

Some of the players were Harvey Pallas, Frank Oles, Bob Wolf, Folmer and Russ Jorgensen. Tom Lyons was the catcher. He said, "We played home games at the House of David park, and every so often Waldo Tiscornia let us use the pristine Ausco park. I don't believe he ever charged us, knowing the team's impoverished position. Waldo came to the games and cheered like mad."

Lyons remembers a couple of innovations to the field installed by Auto Specialties Master Mechanic Bill Unruh. One was a home plate cleaner. This was a pipe running from the nearby Auto's plant to the center of home plate. A metal disc the size of a silver dollar (remember silver dollars?) was set in the center of the plate. When the umpire activated a valve in the ground, air forced the disc up, blowing air and dirt in all directions. The same pipe furnished the force to bring a metal basket filled with new baseballs up from the ground on a four-foot pole. Whenever the umpire ran low on balls, he would step on another valve and the basket would appear.

Note: Tiscornia's mechanized home plate was later donated to the Chicago White Sox Cominsky Park.

Another Baseball Story

In the late 1940s there was a great rivalry between the
St. Joseph Merchants and the Flying Dutchmen of Holland, Michigan. Both teams excelled and their games
drew large crowds. The Dutchmen had one of the first
lighted ball fields for night games. The Auscos had the
only other lighted park.

Russ Jorgensen was pitching, and Lyons was catching
during one night game in Holland—admittedly not one of
Lyons' best efforts—when a Dutchmen batter hit a towering fly ball midway between home plate and the pitcher's
mound. Lyons ran out throwing away the catcher's mask
and searching the sky for the ball. He lost it in the lights
and ran around in a ten foot circle at least three times
trying desperately to locate the ball which finally landed
in the center of his circle and then bounced out across the
foul line. The sight of Lyons staggering around made
Jorgensen laugh so hard he had trouble pitching.

Later in the same game, a high foul ball was hit near the
third base line. Again, Lyons threw off the mask and
raced toward the ball which was soaring near one of the
wooden light poles on the sidelines. As the ball grazed the
pole, Lyons ran up against it and the ball slid down and
lodged inside his chest protector. It was considered a
caught ball and the batter was out. But there was a
player on third who, seeing the circumstances, broke for
home plate. Lyons' recovery of the ball was too late and
he was subject to much good-natured kidding from the
crowd. (Some of it in Dutch!)

How Betty Theisen Helped
Ron Taylor Graduate

When Ron Taylor was a senior at St. Joseph High School,
he dreamed of driving race cars for a living. As graduation approached in 1954, so did Memorial Day and the
Indy 500 race at Indianapolis, Indiana.

Taylor already had connections in the racing world, and
had obtained two tickets to the Victory Dinner as well as
passes to the race. He invited his classmate, Fred
Findeisen, and the two drove to Indianapolis in Fred's
venerable 1949 Ford.

They had a great time watching Bill Vukovich win the
race, and were celebrating at the Victory Dinner in the
Claypool Hotel with other racing enthusiasts. Wilbur
Shaw, three-time Indy 500 winner and Speedway president, presided over the head table and the microphone.

Shaw interrupted the proceedings when a note was
passed to him from a messenger. He read over the amplifying system, "Ron Taylor, please call this number."

Taylor was startled. Had someone died? The number
wasn't to his home telephone. Despite fears of the unknown, he rose with bravado and said to Findeisen,
"That's not the last time you'll hear my name at a victory
dinner."

The number turned out to be that of Betty Theisen or
"Miss T" as her students called her. She was a speech and
drama teacher at SJHS, and had been Taylor's shorthand
and typing instructor.

Noticing the absence of the two students and understanding Taylor's zeal for the track, she was able to locate the boys. Theisen informed Taylor that if he and Findeisen didn't show up for baccalaureate services the next day, they would not be allowed to graduate with their class.

"I've spoken to Mr. Mackay [principal] and you absolutely will not graduate if you are not here for the ceremonies tomorrow," she explained.

Taylor quickly calculated the time necessary to make it back to St. Joseph in time for the service. Then he went back to the table and finished dinner.

In the wee hours of the morning, he and Findeisen burned rubber all the way home. They pulled into Taylor's driveway in Higman Park at about six o'clock in the morning with enough time to shower, change clothes and check in at the high school for baccalaureate.

Miss T was relieved to see them. They graduated on schedule with their class. And, Taylor's words at the victory dinner came true; his name was mentioned again years later when an Indy car he co-owned finished sixth and all of the owners were recognized.

*   *   *

Taylor recalls how he and Miss T became friends. At the urging of his father, Taylor enrolled in shorthand and typing classes to facilitate his studies at college. Miss T was the teacher, and Taylor was a struggling student.

One afternoon, she called him into her office and said, "Ron, I'm going to make you a deal. You're heading into the end of the semester with a strong 'E.' Since I don't want you to fail, if you'll transfer out of shorthand and typing into speech and drama, I'll give you a 'D.'"

That sounded good to Taylor, and he made the switch. As it turned out, he was adept at speech and drama which later helped him with his career in law and politics.

"There's no doubt in my mind that Betty Theisen's decision was a turning point toward my career. Her classes in speech and drama led me into summer stock, and then into radio and television. In law, I was drawn to litigation by my interest in speech and drama. It all cascaded from that point," Taylor said.

He laughs when he recalls that semester in typing. "We used to learn one or two letters a day," he said. "I was sick the day we learned 'Q' and 'P.' To this day, when I use the computer at the courthouse, I have trouble with those letters."

Full Circle

Ron Taylor's decision to pursue a career in law and politics was more than a dream come true for Taylor's father, Russell, an attorney. While Ron was still in college in the early 1960s, his father ran for circuit court judge and was narrowly defeated by the former prosecuting attorney, Karl F. Zick.

Chester Byrns served as Taylor's campaign manager and later ran for circuit court judge on his own. Byrns was elected and sat on the bench with Zick.

When Byrns retired, Ron Taylor decided to run for the position. When the filing deadline of June 5, 1984 arrived without an opponent filing against him, he and his father shared a bottle of champagne.

After a long illness, Russell Taylor died on June 24, 1984 before he actually saw his son elected to the job he had aspired to some twenty years earlier. One can only assume that Russ Taylor passed away content with the knowledge that an important part of his life had come full circle.

Ronald J. Taylor is a lifelong resident of Benton Township. He is married to the former Nancy Hoffius, and is the Chief Circuit Court Judge for Berrien County.

Jack Engelhardt, G.J. "Bic" Bikel, Ron Taylor and Larry Alexander at the Indy 500.

Leon Benson and the Rhythm Ramblers

Georgia Leonard remembers the anticipation of a new shopping center in Benton Township that filled an empty field with grandeur. The words "Fairplain Plaza" had been in the newspaper, on the radio and on the lips of area residents for months. To people who were used to shopping in cozy downtowns, the plaza was a new concept. Imagine walking from store to store and still being protected from the weather by a roof that completely covered the sidewalk!

In June of 1958, plaza organizers planned a gala evening to celebrate the growth of the Twin Cities. The twenty acre parking lot was nearly filled with vehicles as people from around the area gathered for a closer look at the huge plaza.

A flat-bed wagon had been converted into a temporary stage for country entertainer, Leon Benson and his band "The Rhythm Ramblers." A crowd gathered when the "Governor," as Benson was called, took the stage dressed in white western apparel and the band began playing their radio theme song:

Come on and turn your dial around,
The Rhythm Ramblers are back in town.
Stop a while and try to smile.
A smile is better than a frown.

When the theme song was completed, Benson raised his hands into the air for attention. The crowd, which had been singing along with the band, grew silent.

"Hello, everybody," Benson said in a conspiratorial voice. "I'm going to tell you a secret. A very special guest has promised to be here tonight. I know you'll love her, and I want you all to make her feel welcome."

Just then, a disturbance broke out at the rear of the audience. A large, heavyset older woman was trying to elbow her way through the crowd. To make matters worse, she was clutching a guitar in one fist and using it to gently prod people out of her path. The poor old soul plodded along as if each of the knee-high boots she was wearing weighed fifty pounds. She was dressed in a baggy, faded cotton dress tied with a rope instead of a belt. Her gray hair was nearly covered with a ragged babushka knotted beneath her chin.

A ripple of laughter broke out when the elderly woman signaled for help. She wanted to climb onto the stage. Still clutching her guitar in one hand, she managed to scramble up with assistance from two sturdy band members.

She turned to Benson with tears in her eyes and cried, "I'm sorry I'm late Mr. Benson, but that old policeman wouldn't let me ride my horse and I had to walk all the way across this big parking lot all by myself. I'm just plumb wore out."

Benson was sympathetic. He said, "So the big policeman wouldn't let you ride your horse. Where did you leave him?"

"Way over there," she blubbered, pointing to the far end of the parking lot. With Benson comforting her, she brightened a bit and rubbed one fist over her eyes, smearing her caked-on mascara. "Can I still sing with you?" the woman asked shyly.

Benson took her hand and turned her toward the audience. Addressing the increasing crowd, Benson said, "Okay everyone, I promised you a very special guest tonight. I know you're going to love her. Please give Miss Chlorine Waters a hand."

The audience seemed stunned into silence. Some walked away. With encouragement from band members, Miss Waters adjusted her microphone and began singing with Benson. They did a song made famous by the Grand Old Opry duo, Kitty Wells and Red Foley.

Benson sang, "You and me, together, life's a pleasure."

Waters came in on the female part, "But without your love I want to flee."

The audience listened with renewed interest. It was a good imitation of Wells and Foley.

The song was going well when Waters seemed to lose interest in it. She wandered away from her microphone and faced the audience, snickering and pointing at Benson.

He continued singing and it didn't take long for the audience to realize that he had been singing both parts all along, while Waters only lip-synched her part. Benson coaxed her back to center stage and she performed a quick strip-tease. Without the baggy dress, gray wig and babushka, Chlorine Waters turned out to be a long-legged, tall Sheriff's deputy named Tom Kimbro.

This act proved to be so popular that Benson repeated it many times on stages throughout southwestern Michigan. He performed with many partners, sometimes taking the female role himself.

Georgia Hill Leonard and Leon Benson were married for nearly 25 years before his death on April 6, 1968. They spent much of their married life in St. Joseph.

Left to right: Tom Kimbro wearing a dress, Leon Benson in white.

Bob Hope in Berrien County

In the early 1980s Bob Hope entertained at the Berrien County Youth Fair. He stayed at the Benton Harbor Holiday Inn and they directed him to Wyndwicke (now The Oaks) on Niles Road in St. Joseph to practice putting and use the driving range.

Sandy Landis, then owner of the Pro Shop with her husband, Doug, was working that evening with Chris Rose. There were people in the shop and a women's league was waiting to play.

The door opened and in walked a little man. Landis looked at him and thought, "Oh no, it can't be." She recognized him like she would her own father. It was Bob Hope. She stared at him as he very quietly asked her for some range balls. She stood frozen to the spot and couldn't remember where the balls were kept.

Finally, Rose handed Hope a bucket of balls. Both of them stared at him as he walked out the door. No one else in the shop realized who had been there. Rose and Landis ran to the windows and watched him from a distance.

When others noticed Hope on the driving range, they too watched him. But everyone gave the famous entertainer his privacy. Many of the observers were aware that Hope was playing in a Pro-Am Tournament later in the week.

That night at the fair, Hope said he had played golf at "Wind-Wickey" and that he had been treated very nicely.

Sandra Landis has lived in the area for more than 40 years. She taught school in Lakeshore and in St. Joseph. She and Doug owned and ran the Pro Shop at Wyndwicke from 1978-1983. They opened Landis Clothing Company in 1984 in downtown St. Joseph.

A True Fishing Story...Honest

A few years ago, when the now famous salmon fishing was just blossoming on Lake Michigan, Walter Browe agreed to take Harold Andrus on a fishing expedition. Browe was an experienced angler and Andrus had never done this type of fishing, so a crash course on catching, hooking, playing and netting "the big one" took place as they cruised in approximately 40 feet of water north of the piers near Jean Klock Park.

Andrus was a quick and enthusiastic learner. Soon, they were trolling with downriggers, spinning gear and flashy lures. "See where the low sandy beach of Jean Klock Park meets the rising hill of Higman Park, Harold?" Browe asked with an innocent smile.

Andrus nodded and stared at the spot.

"That's where we'll catch our first fish, so get ready," Browe said with conviction. "We're about 100 yards away now. I'll start counting so you'll be prepared...90...80...60...are you ready, Harold?"

"Yes!" he said and rose to his feet.

"50...40...30...stand by, Harold, ready for action!"

Andrus moved closer to the four rods wondering which one would take the strike. Browe kept counting, "Ten, nine, eight, seven, six, five...get ready...four, three, two, one, NOW!"

Truth be told—and Browe promised he'd take a polygraph test—exactly when he yelled "NOW!" a good-sized Coho salmon struck. Andrus grabbed the rod and Browe continued yelling directions in stunned disbelief. Within minutes, they had the fish on ice.

Without missing a beat, Browe decided to attempt this mini-miracle again. "All right, Harold," he said, still shocked but enjoying his luck and the game more than ever. "We're going to turn about and go back over the same spot. There are lots of fish out there just waiting for us."

Andrus moved closer to the rods.

Browe began counting again. "Ten, nine, eight, seven, six, five, four, three, two, one...NOW!"

A fish struck exactly when Browe yelled "NOW!" for the second time. Andrus reeled in a large Chinook salmon while Browe watched in amazement.

The story did not end with two fish. Browe made three more passes over the same spot and Andrus pulled in a different species of Lake Michigan fish each time. They added a Steelhead, a Lake trout and the rare Brown trout to their cooler.

It took Browe a week or so before he had enough nerve to tell the story. He noticed his listeners gasping and trying to maintain expressions of credibility when he reached the punch line. He began to wonder himself if the event had been a dream until, months later, a mutual friend mentioned that Andrus had had a great time fishing with him.

Browe seized the opportunity. He inquired, "Tell me, what did Harold tell you about that day?"

The friend repeated the story almost word-for-word. It wasn't a dream. It really happened...honest!

*This story was submitted by **Dr. Walter F. Browe** who resides in Stevensville with his wife Jean. He was president of Lake Michigan College in 1978-1985. Since then, he served as interim president at four other community colleges. Harold Andrus is an executive at the Whirlpool Financial Corporation.*

Judy Lee II

Gene Siskel at the Curious Kids' Museum

The Curious Kids' Museum opened in downtown St. Joseph in September, 1989. During its first year of operation in the Memorial Hall Building at 415 Lake Boulevard, some 50,000 visitors experienced the hands-on exhibits.

Among these were Chicago film critic Gene Siskel and his family. They happened to arrive at the entry door during a capacity period when prospective visitors are asked to return in 30 minutes or an hour, depending upon the crowd. The Siskels obliged by taking a short walk. When they returned, the volunteer working at the door still didn't recognize Siskel, but even if she had, museum policy states that everyone is given an equal opportunity to learn.

Mary Baske *founded the museum in 1989 to give the children in our communities the same access to learning and experimenting that children in bigger cities have.*

Note: *Read* On the Banks of the Ole St. Joe *for more information on the Curious Kids' Museum and Memorial Hall.*

"Helldamn-Helldamn"

David M. Peterson II, son of Judge David and Marilyn Peterson of St. Joseph, played varsity football in his junior and senior years at St. Joseph High School. One day after football practice, Marilyn recalls her son telling about a team meeting called by Coach Ike Muhlenkamp to "discuss some things."

Marilyn asked what was discussed. Her son replied, "One thing was language. Ike says we can say 'hell' and 'damn' when we get mad, but that's all. So now when we get really mad, we say 'helldamn-helldamn.'"

David M. Peterson II graduated with St. Joseph's class of 1991.

St. Joseph High School

"It is good to be a part of life. Just as a sun-dial counts only the sunny hours, so does life know only that it is living."

H.G. Wells

W. Living

Captain Kidd and John King

Not many of us can trace our genealogy back to the 16th century. In the notes below, Ira King relates the harrowing adventure of how his ancestors came to be in this country. Following is a verbatim account:

"In 1565 during the Huguenot persecutions in France many of the Lascelles (sic) family fled to England. A Lancelles girl married a Pierce and their daughter married a King. Several of these King sons came to New England, but one son remained in London.

"Then came the Black Death and wiped out the whole family except a small boy named John King. His Uncle John King of Weymouth, Mass. made arrangements to have the boy sent to him. The child's way was paid. But the unscrupulous captain sailed to Providence instead and represented that he had brought the youth over at his own expense and bound him out for a considerable sum.

"The child fell into good hands and was trained as a seaman. In due time he became an officer under Captain Kidd. This was while Kidd was acting as a legal buccaneer to keep the ocean free of piratical craft.

"Records that seem trustworthy show that John King left Capt. Kidd and went on board The Adventure." *In 1695 Capt. Kidd was commissioned to clear the West Indian waters of pirates. He turned pirate himself and captured the boat on which John King was serving. As a previous officer under Capt. Kidd, John King was given a choice of joining up or walk-*

ing the plank. He chose to join up. But according to his son, Magdalen, who preserved in writing some of his father's adventures, he was only waiting for an opportunity to escape. That opportunity came in Algiers.

"He passed himself off as a Frenchman and crossed to Marseilles. There he met a French woman and married her. Their only child was Magdalen King, a son."

The notes continue to list several generations of Kings as Ira King traces the descendents of Magdalen's three sons. Among them is **George Glade,** *who was born and raised in the Eau Claire area, and shared these notes with us. Ira King was born in 1857 and buried in Crystal Springs Cemetery in 1925.*

Left to right: Ira King, Lewis Glade holding George Glade.

The Josephine Morton Memorial Home

The Morton Home is a treasured masterpiece since it is
the only house museum in Berrien County. With its
grand white columns rising two stories above a manicured
lawn, the historic home cum museum offers a glimpse into
the past.

If the writing desks, leather books and stereopticon on display in the Morton Home are used as clues, one might deduce that the period between the mid-1800s to the early 1900s was a gracious and quiet time to live.

In the parlor is a working Victor victrola that likely was played by J. Stanley Morton to entertain his wife Carrie and their four children. Its carved wooden cabinet is filled with a record collection carefully indexed—in all probability by Carrie or J. Stanley—in precise handwriting. This forerunner of CD players was made in 1908 by the Victor Talking Machine Company at a cost of $200. Its logo, "Nipper," the white dog listening to his master's voice is now used by RCA. (Remember when they were called RCA Victor?)

Miriam Pede, tour guide chairperson, cranked up the victrola and placed the silver needle on a scratchy rendition of "Columbia, the Gem of the Ocean." The voice of Harry Macdonough filled the air with sounds from days of yore.

We stood on Persian rugs surrounded by a magnificent carved piano with scarf, crystal chandeliers and oil portraits of the Mortons. As refracted light from beveled and stained glass windows cast colorful shadows into the spacious room, we felt for just a moment how they might have felt on a sunny afternoon in the 1900s.

Once nicknamed the "Indian Hotel," the house was built in 1849 by Eleazer Morton—J. Stanley's grandfather—who was the first Caucasian to settle on land that is now known as Benton Harbor. He originally built a log cabin on the present day site of the Liberty Theater on what is now Main Street. As a minority of one, Morton—like the character in the movie *Dances with Wolves*—was always hospitable to the native Potawatomis.

According to Pede, papooses bound to boards were frequently seen leaning up against trees in the yard while their mothers sold baskets in town. The Mortons loaned buffalo robes to those who needed to spend the night on the porch, and the nickname "Indian Hotel" was coined as a result.

The romantic concept of quiet and peaceful living diminishes somewhat when the following elements are considered:

• In the beginning, language was a barrier between Morton and the Potawatomis

• There were no nearby trading posts

• Food had to be shot and skinned before it could be cooked and eaten

• The house was built without indoor plumbing or electricity

• Henry's wife, Josephine—for whom the museum is named—died in childbirth at the age of 29. J. Stanley was the only one of their three offspring to live to adulthood.

Located on the old Territorial Road directly on the route between Detroit and Chicago, the house in the mid-1800s was about half a day's journey from St. Joseph's harbor. (The same trip today, by car, takes about five minutes.)

The home was constructed on land known as the Morton 500-acre farm; its address today is 501 Territorial Road. The wooden house has an oak timber frame with some supporting pieces measuring eight inches square. J. Stanley remodeled the entire house in 1912, supplying a new foundation, raising the roof and ceilings and installing hardwood floors throughout the house. He also installed running water and electricity.

The house sheltered four generations of Mortons before J. Stanley deeded the home to the Benton Harbor-St. Joseph Federation of Women's Clubs in 1942 as a memorial to pioneers.

Volunteers have worked room by room to restore and maintain the home for tours. On display in the 1895 library are glass and wood cases of embossed leather books owned by the Mortons. The family library, typical of the 1890s, includes a variety of volumes on agriculture, gardening, home economics and science as well as sets of writings by Emerson, Poe and many others. In the late 1800s, books were sold by door-to-door salesmen who, judging from the quality of the library, must have regarded the Mortons as valued customers.

A 1912 tub and sink highlight a bathroom decorated with authentic decor from the early 1900s. Volunteers replaced broken tiles in a shell design with replicas made by St. Joseph artist Betty Bingham. The windows are opaque decorative glass. A shoe shine kit and 1920s scale now rest on the floor after having given long years of service.

Sliding pocket doors divide the rooms, and a graceful bird's-eye maple staircase ascends to the second floor where a country bedroom from the 1850s features a rope bed, rag rugs and hand-stenciling. Another bedroom has been redesigned from the Empire Transitional Period of 1830 to about 1855. There is a late-1800s child's room filled with wooden toys, dolls and books from the period and a turn-of-the-century sewing room with an embroidered crazy quilt made from scraps of fabric too precious to discard.

Fabric was cherished by pioneer families. It was redyed, remade and reused until it was a rag unsuitable for anything else. When it got to the point of really being a rag, it was rewoven into rug strips and used for floor coverings. This practice was sound in terms of recycling, but it was also a necessity due to the scarcity of cloth and the long process of spinning and weaving.

The image of gracious living falters again when one considers the early 1900s laundry room reconstructed in the Morton House. In some homes, this area might have been in a kitchen or in a shed where water could be heated. The Morton laundry room sports such "timesaving" appliances as a hand wringer, wash tubs and irons. Soiled fabric was scrubbed by hand with a bar of soap and a wash board. Worn, but not soiled, clothing was aired outside on clothesline. The never-ending nature of dirty laundry—especially with this labor intensive process— makes one wonder when the women of the house had time to read the lovely books in the library.

Federation volunteers, led by President Bea Payne, open the home for free tours on Sundays (2-4 p.m.) and Thursdays (1-4 p.m.) from mid-April through October. Vivian Herkner and Denise Reeves co-chair the museum committee, taking care of the myriad household matters intrinsic to the care of a 142-year-old house. Herkner was on the original committee formed in 1963 by the federation to change the house from a meeting place for clubs and parties to a museum for southwest Michigan memorabilia.

Recognized by the State of Michigan as an historic structure, the house and the Morton family are an integral part of local history in the twin cities of St. Joseph and Benton Harbor. J. Stanley compiled an early history of the area which was published by the Federation of Women's Clubs and entitled *Reminiscences of the Lower St. Joseph River Valley.* It was printed by the A.B. Morse Company of St. Joseph. Volumes are scarce, but the Maud Preston Palenske Memorial Library at 500 Market Street in St. Joseph has copies.

The book discusses such topics as the controversial Fort St. Joseph which Morton places—along with many other reputable historians—in Niles, Michigan.

One chapter details the lifestyles of local pioneers. Morton wrote, "Many a pioneer coming alone into the forest to clear land for a home...spent his first winter in a shelter made of poles and branches just large enough to keep his bed dry..." When the pioneers built permanent cabins, Morton said, "Often the first door was a blanket hung at the opening." And—like *Dances with Wolves*—early settlers told of "wolves nosing aside the blanket at night and, frightened at the fire, slinking away."

Pioneer Lifestyles and
Log Cabins of Southwest Michigan

Virginia Handy comes by her love of log cabins naturally.
Among the Pipestone Township settlers in the 1850s were
her ancestors, the William Tennant family of Glasgow,
Scotland, and the Evans brothers from Wales who became
the namesakes of Evans Road east of Eau Claire.

*Left to right: Three Evans broth-
ers: Thomas, Abraham and David.
There were 12 siblings in this
family.*

Thomas Evans, born in 1828, lived to the ripe old age of
76. His nephew, Charles Kendall, remembered that
Evans once accomplished the feat of splitting 600 rails in
one day. Then, to round out a day's work, he constructed
a worm fence around his yard with the rails.

Thomas' brother, Richard, moved a little to the west and pioneered what became the Vern Deaner farm in Sodus Township. The third brother, Abraham, Handy's great-grandfather, was born in 1838 on a ship crossing the Atlantic. He married Mary Kirkpatrick Tennant, the sister of Joseph Tennant who was elected sheriff of Berrien County in 1904. Tennant served two terms as sheriff.

Abraham and Mary lived in a log cabin on their farm in Pipestone Township. When he enlisted in the Civil War in 1861, she accompanied him and helped in the battlefields with cooking, mending and nursing until they returned from the war in 1863. They produced nine children including Handy's grandmother, Euranie, who married Edward C. Edwards. In 1904, soon after their marriage, the couple was given a farm in Sodus Township by his uncle, Rock S. Edwards. Today the property is owned by Handy's mother, Mary Edwards Handy.

Virginia Handy depicted the Edwards Centennial Farm in a needlepoint which is part of the permanent collection of the 1839 Courthouse in Berrien Springs.

Berrien County jury, circa 1895. Deputy Sheriff Joseph
Tennant is standing at left next to Rock S. Edwards,
owner of the farm pictured in Handy's needlepoint.

With this well-documented background to spur her on,
Virginia Handy has become a pioneer of sorts herself. She
is the founder and mainstay of the Log Cabin Society of
Michigan which was organized in 1988 to sponsor an
annual Log Cabin Day. Governor James J. Blanchard
signed a bill on June 15, 1989 to make Michigan the only
state with an annual statewide festival for the recognition
of log cabins.

A log house owner herself, Handy's home was built with
tulip poplar trees cut down in Russ Forest, a 620-acre
forest preserve in Cass County. The log work on her
home, supervised by Joe Biek, was accomplished using a
scribe to draw saddle notches to fit the log below. Each

log was measured and set individually to insure snug fittings.

"It would have been much easier to build a log cabin using a kit, and many people prefer this method," said Handy, whose home in Sodus Township materialized one and a half years from the time the trees were cut. "But there is nothing more satisfying than to design and create something using natural materials and your own labor."

Handy's cabin is furnished with flax, cotton and wool curtains that she created on her spinning wheels and looms. She said, "My home is a testimonial to my belief that nature is the best inspiration."

Another of Berrien County's log cabins is the 1830s Murdock Log House built by Francis Murdock, an attorney who moved from Maryland to Berrien Springs in 1830. The original basement featured a hidden crawl space where people could hide from attackers. This home is being preserved by the 1839 Courthouse Museum and was moved there in 1974 from its original site off Kephart Lane. As one of the oldest two-story log houses in Michigan, it is open for self-guided tours during the museum's regular hours.

The 1830s Murdock Log House behind the 1839 Court-house in Berrien Springs. Photo by Virginia Handy.

In 1990 the Murdock House was the only place in the United States where the 150th anniversary of William Henry Harrison's "Log Cabin and Hard Cider" presidential campaign was observed. The 1840 campaign became famous for songs, stump speeches, parades of log cabins on wheels, and slogans such as "Tippecanoe and Tyler, Too" and "Keep the Ball Rolling" (illustrated by a huge ball pushed down the street in front of a brass band). Hard cider was in plentiful supply during the campaign, and Harrison won the election but died one month after being inaugurated. Under Handy's guidance, the commemorative event took place at the fourth annual Log Cabin Day celebration which traditionally occurs on the last Sunday in June.

The Jakway Log Cabin was originally constructed in 1835 at the junction of Blue Creek and the Paw Paw River on property later owned by the House of David. Its builder, Richard Lysaght, was an Irishman who served in the British Militia in India, emigrated to Canada, then moved here in the 1830s and married Catherine Yore.

The cabin was moved circa 1890 to Benton Township property owned by Rep. James J. Jakway, a state legislator and later a Benton Township supervisor. Farmers and trappers lived there, and during the early 1940s the cabin was the home of Ojibway Chief Levi Dodge and his family.

Jakway's grandson, James Culby, took over the farm in 1945. Culby and his wife, Jean, restored the cabin and furnished it with pioneer artifacts brought here in 1839 in a covered wagon by his ancestors, Ebenezer and Belinda Jenks Jakway.

Jean Culby projects the demeanor of days gone by as she sits in front of the 1835 Jakway Log Cabin near Benton Harbor which she restored with her husband, James. Photo by Virginia Handy.

The Hoyt Log Cabin circa 1900 was built for Mr. and Mrs. Elwell Hoyt in Eau Claire as a replica of an 1840 log house. Although the cabin no longer exists, a limestone monument carved in the form of a log cabin was erected for the Hoyts in the Eau Claire cemetery.

This grave marker in the Eau Claire cemetery immortalizes the Hoyt's devotion to the log cabin lifestyle. Photo by Carole Kiernan.

Dan Schnitta didn't realize he would own the oldest log cabin on its original site in Michigan when he bought a farm in Berrien Springs. The 1830s Storick log cabin, located over a hill from the farmhouse Schnitta occupies, had a barn built around it.

Storick moved to Berrien Springs in about 1835 and built the cabin with an ax and other simple tools circa 1837, a time when there were no saw mills in the area. A spring near the cabin allowed Storick to live in the cabin all year. "Why he wanted to do that is anybody's guess," said Schnitta, who owns Gingerman Tavern near Wrigley Field in Chicago. "The cabin is in the middle of a field and completely isolated, just like it was when Storick bought the property for about $50 in the 1830s. I'm told he lived alone with the local Indians for several years before taking a wife."

When Schnitta discovered the cabin, he hired Ron Vorrath and Sons of Buchanan to restore it. They took it apart piece by piece, photographed the process, numbered the parts and put it back just like it was. "There is nothing artificial in the house or on the site," Schnitta said. "We used trees on the property and didn't bring in anything foreign to the setting. It's nice. I just let it be."

At the age of 18, Warren Seabury and his 15-year-old brother built a Sassafras log cabin next to a pond near Covert to do the family laundry. "We built it over the water. In fact, the front door is on a pier. But the foundation wasn't sound, and the cabin sagged," said Seabury, now age 61. "In 1982, my son and I decided to restore it for nostalgia's sake. There was so much wrong with it, the restoration turned out to be a rebuilding."

Seabury's labor of love started out to be a getaway cabin for him and his wife Cecelia; it is now a rental home. They added all of the modern conveniences and, like many log home owners, concealed them to maintain the rustic quality.

At the Beehive Farm in Gobles, Nancy and Allen Cassada have a "pretend pioneer family" on their property. The "family" cleared trees to plant crops and build a log house. In 1850, early families took their trees to a sawmill 16 miles away to have lumber cut for their homes. Logs for this cabin were hewed with broad axes and adzes by Al Cassada and some helpers.

The cabin was constructed with square nails like black-smiths once used. "There's a story behind these nails," explained Nancy, who tours the farm with an Australian sheep dog trailing at her heels. "The settlers brought nails with them from the east because often there were no blacksmiths in the territory. If they decided to move on, they would burn their house down and rake the ashes for the nails."

Old wavy glass is fixed into the cabin windows. "If the pioneers were lucky, they'd bring glass with them," Nancy said. "They'd also bring nails, seeds, rope and clippings from plants."

Inside the cabin, the log door is hinged with wooden pegs. A crude slabwood table runs parallel to the fireplace. Handmade chairs hang from pegs on the walls. Across the room a rope bed is covered with a patchwork crazy quilt made from scraps. Two porcelain "thunder mugs" are kept underneath the bed, and a clothing trunk is at the foot. A sleeping loft for children is overhead.

The cabin is approximately 16 by 20 feet, minuscule by any standards. "This is the size cabin that a family of eight might have lived in," said Nancy. "The homesteaders were not rich people. Their homes were crowded. That's why the chairs are hanging on pegs. They only brought a few furnishings with them."

Ben Franklin wrote about one Count Rumford from England. His job was to travel around New England and advise people how to build fireplaces that didn't smoke. The Cassadas read about Rumford in a library and located his dimensions on how to build a smokeless hearth. It was entirely different from the way it's done now. Despite doubts, the Cassadas followed Rumford's instructions, and their fireplace does not smoke.

Herbs hang from the cabin's open rafters. "They used a lot of herbs in cooking," Nancy said. "They dried a lot of food. Some things were pickled. Of course, without electricity they had no refrigeration. They had to make their own candles. They did everything. I tell the kids 'no television' and they think 'Yeah, but they could go to somebody else's house and watch it.'

"I tell the kids, if the pioneer mom wanted to make a rabbit stew, she'd have to ask dad to take his gun and powder horn and go out hunting," Nancy said. "The kids ask 'Why didn't they just drive to the store?' But there were no stores and no cars."

After the cabin was completed, an outhouse was built. "The pioneers began with the necessities," Nancy said. "The shelter came first, the outhouse later."

Leftover branches were used to construct a fence around their garden, and stumps of some trees became a fence surrounding the homestead. They dug a well. The Cassadas helped the "family" by requesting seeds and information from Cornell University to make their early American garden authentic.

They also obtained a strain of rare corn which was given to settlers by local Indians. The variety was kept intact by a family in Schoolcraft. The seeds procured by the Cassadas had been kept frozen for eight years. They planted the corn in a circle, with squash planted in the center to shade the ground and choke out weeds.

"In the 1830s to 1850s pioneers grew peas and finger potatoes," Nancy explained. "Their radishes were black, and hot! They grew lots and lots of beans because they could store them. Some of the varieties they used were Soldier Beans, Jacob's Cattle and Early Horn."

The garden has rows of Red Pear and Yellow Plum tomatoes, onions, cabbage, field corn, squash and pumpkins. "The early settlers used pumpkins like we use squash," Nancy said. "They grew gourds to use as scoops, bowls and decorations. We plant different crops every year for fun. We want to try growing tobacco. The early Michigan settlers grew tobacco for their own use."

Ida Jager lives in a cozy log house in St. Joseph that is more than 100 years old; it was a gift to her from her brother, Frank Endres. "I don't know much about it, except it's a sturdy house," she said. "It was originally built where the road is now. When the road was constructed, they pushed the house over here."

According to *Log Home Living*, a magazine dedicated to the lifestyle, there are some 250,000 log home owners in this country. Just to drop a couple of big names...H. Ross Perot, author, hero and Texas billionaire owns one, as does country singer Hank Williams, Jr.

Logan J. Drake
A Man Who Lived His Dreams

Colonel J.J. Drake was born in England and moved with his parents to Chicago, then Ohio and finally St. Joseph. Here, he met and married Frances Brewer.

In 1863, when Frances became pregnant with their first child, she and J.J. made an agreement. He would name the child if it was a boy, and she would name a girl. J.J. had two very close friends from the service, General John Logan and General Joseph Hooker. When the baby boy was born, J.J. wanted to name him Hooker. Frances blew a gasket. No way would she allow her child to be named Hooker. She said she never liked Joe Hooker anyway and certainly wasn't going to name a son after him. After much dissention in the Drake household, J.J. gave in and their child, Logan Jay Drake, was named after his other good friend.

* * *

When Logan was about six years old he told his father he couldn't go to school because he was too busy. He wanted to work as a lumberjack, join a circus, build boats and own a playground where children and adults could have fun.

His father said, "Fine, but get an education first."

School and young Logan Drake did not mix, and when the boy was ten years old he ran away from home, hitched a ride to Ludington and went to work in a lumber camp. In those days, circa 1873, people did not worry about runaways or a worker's age. The lumberjacks gave the boy a bunk and paid him 35 cents a day for help around the camp. After about two months time, Logan felt he had accomplished one of his dreams and decided to pursue another.

He hopped a train and rode the rails to Chicago where he wandered, mostly in the Loop, for several days. He began thinking he should go home when he spotted an advertisement for the Barnum & Bailey Circus. The chance to see the circus for free everyday was too much for the young lad to pass up. He asked for directions, found the circus and procurred a job watering elephants. He stayed with the circus for several weeks before leaving, intending to return home.

At the Chicago docks, Logan became enamored with the huge tramp steamers tied there. When no one was looking, he boarded one and hid. His dream to learn about boats and become a boat builder overcame his homesickness and he cruised with the steamer for about three months. In that time he scrubbed decks, washed clothes, cleaned, polished and learned to cook.

When the steamer returned to Chicago, Logan disembarked and hopped a train back to St. Joseph. The young boy who returned home was more worldly than most older boys, but his father still insisted upon an education for his son. To avoid a repeat of the past adventures, Logan was immediately enrolled in the Morgan Park Military Academy where he learned to take orders, drill and study.

* * *

Always industrious, Logan bought and sold a candy business in Chicago with his brother, Fred, and then purchased the 20-22 acres of sand dunes along Lake Michigan which would become Silver Beach in St. Joseph, Michigan. In 1880, at the tender age of 17, Logan bought the beach and also some riverfront property near the railroad tracks. He started a boat construction and livery business before developing the Silver Beach Amusement Park which would become a major attraction in St. Joseph.

*Information for this story was supplied by **Roberta Drake Terrill**, daughter of Logan J. and Maude (Schlenker) Drake. Mrs. Terrill has lived in St. Joseph all her life and ran Silver Beach with her husband H.J. Terrill after her father's death in 1947.*

Note: *Read* On the Banks of the Ole St. Joe *for a complete account of the Silver Beach Amusement Park.*

Dickinson Stadium

In the late 1800s, two Chicago industrialists and brothers, Theodore and William Dickinson, decided to purchase property on the other side of the lake for part-time residences.

Theodore bought the land where St. Joseph High School is now. He developed an estate with a large home, stables, barns, caretaker homes, formal and informal gardens. The Dickinsons had one daughter named Rose.

When her parents died, Rose turned the property over to the city of St. Joseph for public use as an arboretum to be maintained by members of a local garden club.

Later, city leaders designated the property—which had become a centrally located site as the population grew—for use as a contemporary high school. The school opened in 1959 and the stadium was named Dickinson Stadium.

The Dickinson House

*   *   *

The other brother, William, purchased property slightly south of Scottdale. Like his brother, William developed a country estate with a gracious home and outbuildings. It is located on Dickinson Road, named after William, and is the current residence of his granddaughter, Caroline Dickinson Hoffmann Witte, and her husband, Lyle Witte.

William Dickinson traveled from Chicago to St. Joseph by train and was transported from the station to his estate by his coachman, Mr. Green. Green had a son who became Bishop Green and, according to Lyle Witte, was a well-known and loved person in this area.

The Wittes added a large stable and arena to the estate and operated Stockbridge Farms, a riding school and boarding stable, for more than 20 years. Before the school was closed, the Wittes reviewed their roster and found that during their tenure they had trained more than 5,000 students in horsemanship.

William Dickinson donated land, hired an architect and provided funds for the construction of a schoolhouse now located on Niles Road in Royalton Township. Lyle Witte purchased the property from the St. Joseph school district circa 1977. The building is now used as the headquarters for his business, Witte & Associates Interiors.

*Contributed by **Lyle Witte**, a native of Chicago and a resident of St. Joseph for more than 30 years.*

Note: *In 1893 the two blocks of Lakeview Avenue between Main Street (then called Napier) and Howard, were named Dickinson Avenue. In 1906, Dickinson Avenue was changed to Lakeview.*

Jack

Jack, a Boston terrier owned by Stanley Stock, was a familiar sight in downtown St. Joseph. The Stocks lived at the corner of Forres and Winchester, and the streetcar line ran on Winchester. Whenever Jack felt like having ice cream, he would board the streetcar and ride downtown to the Square Drug Store which was located on the northeast corner of State and Pleasant Streets. The owner and Stock were good friends and Jack was always welcome.

In May of 1916, while Jack was downtown, he was stolen and taken to Chicago on one of the Graham and Morton boats. He escaped his captors and found his way to the docks where he spent two days before boarding the *Puritan*.

Jack was immediately adopted by the crew of the Holland bound boat. In Holland, Jack disembarked probably believing he was back home in St. Joseph.

Several days later he again boarded a boat, the *City of Benton Harbor,* and returned to St. Joseph. His adventure lasted six days. Whether he stopped for ice cream and rode the streetcar home is unknown.

*This story was submitted by Stanley Stock's daughter, **Marjorie S. Clemens**, who resides in Benton Harbor and has lived in the area all of her life.*

Sanitary Napkins, Five Cents

When Ruth Gillespie Grootendorst was a little girl, she
loved to go downtown after school and visit her father,
Frank Gillespie, who owned and ran the Gillespie Drug
Store in downtown St. Joseph. She adored him and always looked forward to these visits.

One afternoon, when Ruth was about seven years old, she
arrived at the store and it was quite busy. Frank gave
her some money and suggested she go around the corner
to the YWCA for a snack.

At that time, circa 1917, the YWCA was located upstairs
in the 505 Pleasant Street building and served what was
considered the only "fast" food in town. That is, the food
for sale was prepared by volunteers prior to delivery to
the cafeteria. YWCA volunteers were known to be very
proper ladies, well-respected in the community.

Little Ruth, a proper young lady herself, went into the
restroom to wash her hands before eating. Inside, she
noticed a new machine labeled "Sanitary Napkins, Five
Cents." Ruth thought that was a good idea, and she had a
nickel in her pocket. She pushed her nickel through the
slot and out popped a cardboard box which landed in a
tray at the bottom of the machine. Ruth felt as though
she had received a special gift. She opened the box and
found the napkin and two pins inside. She decided the
napkin was meant to be pinned under the chin like a
trough. So, looking in the mirror to get it on straight, she
attached it to her blouse.

Imagine the thoughts of the YWCA ladies when this
young girl walked out of the restroom wearing a sanitary

napkin on her chest. Ruth remembers the secretaries seemed to fly at her from around their desks to remove it. These items simply were not mentioned in those days, much less shown in public (or worn on one's chest).

In retrospect, Ruth feels sorry for the women who had to wear those napkins. She says it must have been like wearing a hair shirt, for the product then was thick and stiff as a board.

Ruth Gillespie Grootendorst has lived in St. Joseph all of her life. She is the only daughter of Frank and Helen Gillespie and the widow of Andrew Grootendorst.

Ruth, age 3

Early Twentieth Century Sketches

Robert P. Small tells about life in the Twin Cities during the early years of this century from the viewpoint of a child growing up. He remembers nearly every room, stairway, banister, nook and cranny of Columbus School on Columbus Street in Benton Harbor.

Miss Carley in kindergarten wore white islet dresses that reached to her black shoes. She stood in the doorway and greeted her students each morning with a big smile. The kindergarten room had big windows overlooking the playground.

Miss Burridge wore white blouses and long dark skirts. She taught reading with word cards and the chalk board in her first grade classroom. That room was next to the kindergarten room with corridors in between where the children hung their coats on hooks. She directed small plays of stories such as "The Three Billy Goats Gruff" where the children took turns portraying the ogre and the goats.

Across the hall were second and third grades where Miss Griffin began teaching arithmetic in second, and Miss Shoup started geography in third. Small said, "When you moved upstairs to fourth, fifth, sixth and seventh grades you were really growing up. Miss Griffin 'grew up' too, when she became principal and moved upstairs to teach fourth and seventh grades."

Streetcars...

Streetcars ran out of car barns on Main Street in downtown Benton Harbor to destinations such as Fairplain, Hull Avenue, Fair Avenue, the House of David and St. Joseph. These were depicted by signs of the same names on the front of the cars which the motormen would turn and change as needed.

The Benton Harbor-St. Joseph Railway and Light Company was commonly known as the "Traction Company." Its office was in a building called the "Traction Building" which also housed the Red Cross Drug Store and a shop where residents could pay their light bills or buy fixtures.

A ride from Napier Avenue in Fairplain to St. Joseph at Wells Field cost a nickel. Free transfers were included in the price. Small said, "Streetcars saved a lot of walking when you had a nickel."

A popular route was from the Central Dock to the House of David. Cars on that route were loaded to overflowing on weekends when the boats came in from Chicago.

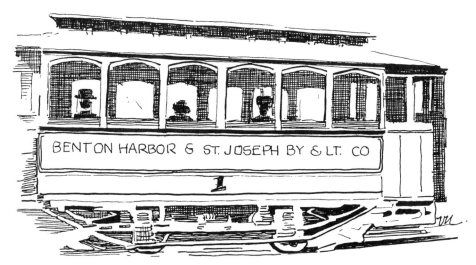

Passengers boarded at the back, paid the conductor and chose a seat in the front, back, middle, right or left sides of the car. As a young lad, Small was fascinated with the view of houses, horses and telephone poles as the cars sailed along the middle of the street. He marveled at the motormen running the cars slowly uphill, clanging the bells and pushing the handbrakes with all their might as the cars descended downhill. He still says, "What a wonder; the streetcars were wonderful things."

Silver Beach...

When Small and his friends went to Silver Beach they took the Fairplain streetcar to downtown Benton Harbor where the motormen changed the sign to "St. Joseph." The car continued across the River Bridge and the Morrison Channel Bridge (now the Bicentennial Bridge), turned at the courthouse and stopped at the lake bluff. He remembers the ride as a holiday in itself.

From the bluff (near the site of today's *Maids of the Mist* fountain), Small recalls the Penny Stairway which he rode once. He and his friends walked down the stairs, past the "Iron Clad Hosiery" (Cooper & Wells) building where the first sight of Silver Beach Amusement Park was the backside of the roller coaster.

The roller coaster was at the park's entrance and across from that was a covered picnic area with tables and benches. A wide, covered boardwalk led to a hamburger stand on the right, followed by a fun house, the dance floor, a car ride on an electric steel floor, a ball-throw at wooden milk bottles, a fortune teller, another ball-throw where the prizes included Kewpie dolls and a rifle shoot at moving targets. On the left from the picnic area were benches, a spun candy stand, more benches, an airplane ride for little kids, a power ride for older ones and the merry-go-round.

The merry-go-round had a facsimile of the elusive brass ring we've all heard about. In this case, catching it was worth a free ride and Small once caught it four times in a row, riding five times for a nickel.

The Fruit Industry...
Farm trucks and wagons loaded with peaches, apples, melons, grapes, tomatoes, cucumbers, squash and more stopped right in the middle of Wall Street for business at the Benton Harbor Fruit Market. People crowded around

the vehicles which lined up one behind the other for blocks. Farmers and brokers haggled and gestured until a sale was made, while children helped themselves to pieces of fruit from the extra bushels on the sidewalks. The sweet smell of the fruit lingered in the air long after the trucks and wagons had pulled away from what was known as the "largest cash to grower non-citrus fruit market in the world."

Fruit buyers often included transportation to the Graham & Morton Docks in their deals with the growers. The fruit then had to be moved manually from the trucks and wagons to the docks, and finally to the holds of boats such as *The City of Grand Rapids, The City of Holland, The City of Benton Harbor, The City of St. Joseph,* and *The City of Saugatuck.* On weekdays these sidewheelers carried fruit and freight to Chicago and transported people back. Weekend excursions carried passengers only.

The Graham & Morton Docks were built on the river between Main Street in downtown Benton Harbor and the ship canal. The docks bordered both the St. Joseph and the Paw Paw Rivers where they join east of the turning basin. Great pilings bound with immense rope and wharf planks as big as trees ran along the river banks. An

approximate width of ten feet of the dock area was open to the weather; the remainder of the wharf was a covered warehouse.

During WWI, in 1917 or 1918 there was a shortage of workers to load fruit onto boats for shipment to Chicago. Small and some of his friends became "wharf rats." He says, "There is nothing sweeter to perfume the air than ripe apples, peaches, melons and grapes. There's nothing heavier than a jumbo basket of melons. And there was nothing nicer than forty cents an hour in our pockets. We worked from the time school was out until dark or later if our work wasn't finished."

He recalls the noise and bustle of activity as the fruit was loaded for shipment to Chicago, and remembers the deserted docks after hours when spooky echos bounced off the empty spaces.

Lake Bluff Park...
In the early years of this century, a wide walkway began on the north end of Lake Bluff Park at the *Firemen's Monument*. The walk curved south to the *Maids of the Mist* fountain and the Penny Stairway and ran parallel to the lake shore. Wooden benches lined both sides of the walk.

Due east of the park, across Lake Boulevard, was the Whitcomb Hotel, the Lakeview Hotel, the Inter-Urban Station and Murphy's Restaurant. Small remembers Murphy as a "five-by-five man who dressed in white shirts and white pants. He shouted to the crowds through a megaphone about the virtues of his eating establishment."

The walkway continued to the intersection of Broad Street and Lake Boulevard where the 1864 cannon pointed toward the lake with mounds of cannon balls on each side. Small remembers winning many a battle playing around the cannon.

The park rises sharply from the river and lake levels below, forming a palisade to downtown St. Joseph. The Big Four brought trainloads of people to St. Joseph on weekends and the park was a favorite gathering spot. Passengers would walk up the Broad Street stairwell to the walkway where the park was planted with grass, trees and shrubbery. People found many excellent places to picnic, snooze, walk or run.

Robert P. Small was born in Benton Harbor in 1907. He was the Prosecuting Attorney for Berrien County in the 1940s and was active in many community activites including serving as president of the Lake Michigan College Board of Trustees, president of the Safety Council, chairman of the Red Cross and the Community Chest, and served on the board of the Berrien Community Foundation. He resides today in Higman Park with his wife, Mary Elizabeth.

House of David Reminiscences

Paul Johnson and Tom Dewhirst recall many times in the 1920s and early 1930s when men and boys of the House of David would gather in recreation rooms located above the boiler rooms in one large building on East Britain Avenue in Benton Harbor which housed a bakery, an electric shop, two engine shops and a plumbing shop.

The members also maintained shops for a tailor, laundry, mill, musical instruments, woodworking, paint, saw filing, framing, shoe repair, souvenirs and art. They ran printing presses, greenhouses, a canning plant, fruit drying and freezing facilities, and a dairy that supplied milk, butter and eggs. They bred and raised horses, made jam and jelly, produced vegetables and fruit, ran an amusement park and local hotels, had a nationally known baseball team and accomplished many other things—some of which are discussed in other sections of this book.

There were no locks on any doors at the House of David. Members might be found in the recreation rooms at any time, day or night, studying the faith, talking or playing checkers and cards. The rooms could hold 100 people and were often filled on Saturdays and Sundays.

Approximately 25 to 30 members would wait for the dinner bell to ring in these comfortable rooms which were kept toasty during winter months by the coal burning boilers located beneath the wooden floors. At these gatherings talk might turn to the day's work, tomorrow's plans or a member's interpretation of the faith.

Perhaps because it is universally true or perhaps because the dinner bell cut the conversation short, someone was bound to end the discussions by saying, "Well, we're all going to get what we deserve in the end."

This story brings to mind a quote from the February, 1990 issue of the *Hope Health Letter*: "Some people who are not paid what they are worth ought to be glad."

*   *   *

Dewhirst also recalls the times in the early 1900s when bathtubs were constructed of wood and the water was heated with steam. The noise and rumblings of the steam going through the plumbing gave House of David members an idea of what the day might sound like when the water returns to the center of Earth. A House of David writing called *The Balls of Fire* speaks of Earth's creation and says that as the North and South Poles melt, water will trickle back into Earth and cause a rumble like steam running into a bathtub. The members believe that the Earth was originally six parts land and one part water, and that the Earth's axis was originally from east to west. The writings say that Earth received a severe jolt that turned the axis to north/south.

According to teachings this will reoccur in a "relatively few years" and the axis will return to east/west as the water recedes. They say that the earthquakes we have had until this time are nothing compared to what will come then.

H. Thomas Dewhirst and Paul Johnson are members of the House of David.

The Dead-End Kids of Morrison Avenue

Jean Schuett Koebel was a "dead-end" kid who maintains many happy memories of her childhood on Morrison Avenue. As a child in the 1920s, Koebel remembers the horse-drawn milk wagons from Producer's Creamery. If the horses trotting by left a memory of their own in front of the Schuett family home, she would call out to her father, "Quick! The horse left some manure on the street." He would grab a shovel and make his wife happy by working the manure into their flower garden.

The iceman from Brown's Coal and Ice always drew a crowd of children when he came down the street. They loved to chomp on slivers of ice that flew from his pick as he chipped ice into blocks to fit the household iceboxes. His wagon was wet and dripping under the canvas covered ice as he stopped and read the signs posted in front windows: "25 Pounds" or "50 Pounds." Then, he hoisted the ice with a pair of tongs, completed the delivery and went on his way.

A path behind the Schuett home led to Kiwanis Park where summer evenings were spent watching the free softball games played by teams from local factories and businesses. The children split their time between the games and the playground equipment, sliding down the big slide and swinging high on the swings.

At the dead end of Morrison Avenue was a streetlight where the youngsters gathered after supper to sit and outdo each other telling spooky stories. Koebel remembers all of the children running home as fast as they could after these sessions, each one filled with his own personal images of the ghosts and monsters from the stories.

On some Saturday mornings, Mr. and Mrs. Emil Klemm of Morrison Avenue would "hire" the children to help them with their custodial duties at St. Peter's Evangelical Church on Church Street. After the benches and chairs in the church were dusted, the children were given a dime for their good work. Ten cents was all it took to produce ear-to-ear grins on their young faces and the money was often spent on the Saturday matinees at the Caldwell Theater on State Street.

At Blossomtime, the Morrison Avenue kids planned their own "blossom parade." Wagons and bikes were decorated and a queen was chosen. In 1930, little Jean Schuett had the honor of being chosen queen. She was awarded a homemade crown, a bouquet of flowers and a seat on the queen's decorated wagon.

"Queen" Jean Schuett Koebel in her decorated wagon was pulled by Henry Meyer in the annual Morrison Avenue "Blossom Parade." Ben Abraham looks on from the background left.

In the early 1930s, for high adventure the neighborhood kids ran to the old State Street bridge to watch boats such as *The Grand Rapids* and *The S.S. Roosevelt* enter the harbor. Unbeknown to the bridge tender, the kids would hop onto the bridge as it swung open and marvel at the river below and the big boats alongside.

The years of 1935 to 1937 were especially memorable for Koebel who worked for the Gillespie family in their drug store. Wearing a blue and white uniform, she was a "soda jerk" who was proud to work in the store that she says, "sold the best sodas and sundaes made with homemade ice cream." After the store closed, Koebel remembers, "we gals went upstairs, off came our uniforms and on went our fun outfits for an evening at the Tip Top Cafe. There we met our friends, played the juke box and ate hamburgers. Those were great evenings on the town."

Jean Schuett Koebel has lived in St. Joseph "the town I dearly love" for more than 70 years.

184

A Penny Saved is a Penny Earned

When Pearl Burkhard Wilcox was a child, she lived with her family at 909 State Street. While playing in Lake Bluff Park, little Pearl noticed one of her neighbors, Mrs. Wallace A. (Mary King) Preston, picking up twigs for her kitchen stove and using her large apron as a carrier.

Pearl timidly approached Mrs. Preston, and asked, "Why are you picking up those sticks when you have all the wood you want at your lumber company?"

Mrs. Preston replied, "My dear, we *sell* every piece of wood at the lumber company."

The Prestons owned Preston Lumber on Main Street in Benton Harbor. They resided at 720 State Street with their children William Arthur, Loomis, Nathan, John, Calvin and Maud Elizabeth. This story was told to Polly Preston Parrett by Pearl's daughter, Mary Wilcox Pielemeier.

Maud and Fred's Family

Fred and Maud Preston Palenske had no children, so they "adopted" the neighborhood children. On Sunday mornings, Fred drove downtown to Carlton & Walters and picked up his regular order of newspapers with comics. These included the *Kansas City Star, St. Louis Dispatch* and papers from Detroit and Chicago.

After Sunday school, there might be eight to ten young readers sprawled on Palenske's living room floor reading the escapades of "Maggie & Jiggs," "Felix the Cat," and "Tillie the Toiler."

An Easter Egg Hunt

The Palenskes also organized an annual Easter Egg Hunt on their property at the corner of Ridgeway and Prospect (now Marina Drive) for all of the Edgewater children who were ten-years-old and younger. This event began in 1928 with four children and continued until World War II.

Through the years, the hunt expanded to include the U.S. Coast Guard families living on the North Pier, North State Street (now Upton Drive) residents, as well as the children living on Ridgeway and Prospect. The numbers of children grew to about 60.

In the last years, some 78 dozen hard-boiled eggs were cooked and colored by members of the First Congregational Church. Polly Preston Parrett remembers one year when the church members neglected to boil half of the eggs—what a mess!

"Uncle" Fred started the hunt by lining up the youngest children in front, the older ones next, and the fastest runners in the back. He shouted, "One, two, three!" and they were off.

Prizes were given to the girl and boy with the most eggs. The child finding the "Golden Goose $Egg" received the best prize which might be a pair of ball-bearing roller skates or a Parker pen and pencil set. Each child went home with six eggs, a sack of candy and an invitation from the Palenskes to return the next year.

*These stories were submitted by **Polly Preston Parrett** who lived on Ridgeway with her parents, John and Phyllis (Wilkinson) Preston.*

More Memories about the Palenskes...

Bruce Ball also remembers the Palenskes and the many wonderful childhood memories they provided. He relates that not only did they give us the Maud Preston Palenske Memorial Library; since they had no children of their own, they were like parents to the neighborhood children.

Ball said, "Every Sunday, Fred would read the funnies out loud while the kids gathered around on the floor looking at the pictures. He and Maud also kept a record of children's heights on the door frame leading into the sun room."

Ball's family films show parents and children all bundled up against the cold lake winds—no one seemed to mind the cold—when the Palenskes held their annual Easter Egg Hunt. "On a signal from Fred, we would charge all over their yard looking for hidden eggs," Ball said. "Each child had a small basket, and supposedly the one with the most eggs won a prize, but everyone seemed to get a little something."

*Information contributed by **Bruce and Margie (Schultz) Ball.***

Note: *The Maud Preston Palenske Memorial Library is located at 500 Market Street in downtown St. Joseph.*

Joe Louis at the Caldwell

Joe Louis, long-reigning heavyweight boxing champion during the 1930s, spent several summers at the home of his manager in Stevensville. Louis was a familiar figure at the Caldwell Theater in downtown St. Joseph where he attended movies several times a week.

Louis always sat in the back row on the left side of the theater. When word of his presence spread around town, a steady stream of children paraded up and down the left aisle just so they could say, "I saw Joe Louis."

According to A. Karl Gast, Louis was also a frequent customer at Frankie's and Johnny's Driving Range on Lake Shore Drive. Frank Lahr and John Crow, St. Joseph High School graduates, ran the enterprise until one summer night when, as the story goes, someone stole all of the golf balls.

*These stories were submitted by **Polly Preston Parrett,** a lifetime resident of St. Joseph. Today, John Crow is a local attorney with the firm Hartwig, Crow and Jones. Frank Lahr is a senior vice president of First of Michigan Corporation in St. Joseph; of Frankie's and Johnny's, he said, "I don't remember closing due to stolen golf balls; I think we had to get real jobs. I do recall that we had to move the 200 yard marker up to 150 yards because the balls became so waterlogged no one could hit them that far."*

Phil D'Andrea's House

Pat and Alan McKee's house has a tunnel in the basement. "We can't see it now because it's been filled in on both sides," said Pat McKee. "I guess it sat empty for a period of time and previous owners were afraid children might play in or near it and get hurt. We can hear the hollowness of the tunnel. Rumor is that if Al Capone or other notorious men were in the house and had to escape in a hurry, they could run through the tunnel to a boat moored on the banks of the St. Joseph River."

McKee's house was built in 1933 by Phillip D'Andrea, one of Capone's body guards. "D'Andrea's take was the Chicago Public Works," said McKee. "People who grew up here remember convoys of trucks coming every Monday from Chicago to build this house."

Also in the basement is a room equipped with closets, shelves and a complete bathroom. "We think this must have been servant's quarters," said McKee. "We've heard that there might have been a wading pool in the basement, too. The architecture lends itself to such a thing, but no documentation has been found."

The living room features a fireplace built of Italian marble from the district where D'Andrea's family began. "Some of the marble steps leading upstairs are attached with screws," said McKee. "It's been said that these steps opened to hide guns."

There is a built-in bookcase that opens on the third floor. "This would have been a dandy place to hide a person," McKee said. "In the same room, the round windows are smaller on the outside than on the inside. It's likely that these were constructed for gun portholes."

Tile work in the bathrooms was done by Pat Golden. "I happen to know Mr. Golden's daughter Kay," said McKee. "She told me stories about her father doing business with D'Andrea. The work he did in the master bathroom was quite a piece of art for the early 1930s. He used black tile which was unusual then. It was patterned after one of Frank Sinatra's bathrooms. Evidently, D'Andrea was either a friend or an admirer of Sinatra."

McKee remembers Kay and her mother, Amy Golden, talking about a birthday party they attended for D'Andrea's son. "Amy's son Bill was the same age as D'Andrea's son. When they arrived at the party, there was a brand new red wagon for Bill identical to the one D'Andrea's son received. Despite the fact that he was a crook, they were good family people."

When D'Andrea was convicted for extortion in 1943, the house was sold to local industrialist Carl Schultz. At that time, the *News-Palladium* reported that the D'Andrea family was quiet but the home had an "air of mystery." The McKees purchased the house in 1983.

Pat and Alan McKee are natives of Muskegon. They have lived in St. Joseph for 24 years. Pat is a former co-owner of Pullover Plus; she currently works in Congressman Fred Upton's campaign office as office manager/volunteer coordinator.

Revenge is Sweet

In 1935 the kindergarten at Jefferson School was held in the large room to the right of the main entrance. It had a marble fish pond built into the floor with kneeling walls on all four sides. Elaine Vanderberg (then Hrach) remembers a classmate, Billy Fleckles, who constantly teased her.

One day opportunity knocked for Elaine to even the score with Billy. As he was leaning on the kneeling wall, Elaine pushed him straight into the pond. She doesn't remember what punishment was levied on her, but Elaine clearly recalls the joy of getting even with a bully and later becoming friends with him.

Today, the kindergarten room is used by the St. Joseph Beauty College and the pond is filled with plants.

Elaine C. Vanderberg has lived here most of her life (except during college and early married years). She is a retired medical technologist and along with her husband Robert owns Uniformly Yours, a retail store in downtown St. Joseph.

A St. Joe Original
by Frank F. Lahr

Joe Stueland graduated from St. Joseph High School in
1939. Among the teachers relieved to see Stueland leave
the premises was Fred Greene, the science teacher.
Greene once cautioned Stueland as he held a bottle of
sulphic acid and Stueland promptly put the bottle to his
lips and drained the contents, falling to the floor in mock
death. Little did the science teacher know that Stueland
had replaced the acid with water and was waiting for this
moment.

Another teacher nearly fainted when Stueland stabbed
himself during an English class and fell to the floor with
the knife sticking out of his chest. This prank was accomplished by placing a board inside his shirt.

In June of 1939, the King and Queen of England were
making a 22-day tour of the United States. Stueland had
some skills as a cartoonist and together with John Crow
and Frank Lahr compiled a one-time, one-page paper
called *The Informer.* They rebuked the royal couple for
snubbing the Twin Cities on their tour and urged a boy-
cott of English toffee, Canada Dry ginger ale and London
tweeds, along with a program to shoot all English spar-
rows. One cartoon in the paper depicted the United
States with Michigan and St. Joseph in capital letters.
New York and Chicago were mere dots on the map. Seven
hundred copies of *The Informer* were placed in mailboxes
in the area.

While still in high school Joe went swimming in Lake
Michigan in the middle of winter. He had to climb out
about 100 yards from shore before the ice on the lake was

open enough to jump in—all this to accept a dare. Later, he became a member of the Polar Bear Club of Chicago.

Stueland's Army Air Corps career was distinguished by an aversion to anyone with a rank higher than PFC. He was too much a free spirit for the military.

After the war, Stueland joined his father, Fritz, at F.N. Stueland Electrical Contractors. While doing some work near a ceiling duct at the old Peoples State Bank, Joe was working with a tool that used .22 cartridges to attach fasteners. Amplified by the duct work, this tool sounded like a rifle shot. Joe, who had a slight stutter, shouted into the duct, "This is a st-st-stick up." John Stubblefield, the dignified founder and president of the bank, was an unlikely foil for Joe's humor, but strangely enough was one of his friends.

Stueland was a small boat sailor of some renown. For several years he reigned as the leading spirit of the Lightning Fleet, usually battling Bill Campbell for the fleet championship. He trailed his boat all over the Midwest where everyone knew him and everyone had a "Stueland" story. In one race he sailed in a heavy fog off of Chicago. The boats couldn't see each other or the buoys. Stueland was in first. At the clubhouse he was describing his tactics using "chaotic"—one of his favorite words—but he couldn't keep a straight face and finally confessed, "Aw heck, I didn't go around any buoys."

Another time in Chicago a group of sailors was attending a play and Stueland was in a loge. As the usher closed the curtain, Stueland spoke up in his deep voice that could be heard throughout the theater and said, "Let me out of here, Lincoln was shot in a seat like this."

Stueland's other love was flying. Combining these loves led to a tragic accident. While flying to a regatta in the Bahamas in March of 1969 with his wife, Shirley, their sons, Scott and Jeff, and Ricky Crow, Stueland's plane crashed into a hillside in Tennessee. Ice had built up in the carburetor. All five passengers died in the crash.

Joe Stueland

Frank Lahr is an alumni member of the Lightning Fleet for which Joe Stueland also sailed. Lahr says, "Whenever the graying Lightning Fleet alumni get together, Joe is always with us—his humor and love of sailing ever present."

Lake Court

Although Inez Dumke now lives on Lydia Drive in St. Joseph, 318 Lake Court will always be her special home. She was born and raised in the house, and grew up virtually living on the beach near the St. Joseph Pumping Station.

"The outstanding memory of growing up on Lake Court is the 'boardwalk' at the dead end of the street," she said. "It led to the beach, but two benches halfway down were the meeting place for teenagers. Living where I did, I could see who went to the beach and when they went. It was the catbird seat!"

Lake Court "Boardwalk"

Some fifty years ago, James Dansfield managed the pumping station and also supervised the teenagers, counting heads when they swam and generally keeping an eye on them. Inez grew up with a sense of community security and pride that increased when she brought her own first-born son, Michael, to the house on Lake Court.

Inez R. Dumke has lived in St. Joseph all her life. She is a former home economics teacher in the St. Joseph and Benton Harbor schools, a Sunday school teacher for the First United Methodist Church, and has served as a volunteer for the Boy & Girl Scouts, Service League, Crippled Children and the hospital.

The Cannon Balls
Now You See Them, Now You Don't

The iron cannon next to the Broad Street stairwell bears the date 1864 and was unveiled in St. Joseph on July 4, 1897. Historically, two piles of cannon balls stood on each side of the cannon. Frank Klemm remembers rolling those authentic cannon balls over the bluff for sport along with "many other sand rabbits."

Later, in the 1940s the cannon balls were to be donated to the World War II scrap drive headquartered locally on a site next to the present day Saron Lutheran Church on Main Street. But Frank and his father, Max Klemm, saw the cannon balls in Max Jafke's junkyard on the current site of Whitcomb Tower's parking lot at State and Port Streets. Somehow they never made it to the federal scrap collector, and Frank remembers Jafke stating that the cannon balls were the ones from Lake Bluff Park.

Frank Klemm has lived in the twin cities area throughout his life, and has worked for Gast Manufacturing Corporation for 22 years.

* * *

After approximately 45 years of absence, the cannon balls were restored to their former site beside the cannon. In 1989 and 1990 St. Joseph resident Fred Krause sold cannon balls for $60 each to individuals and businesses who now have their names imprinted on the balls. The cannon balls were cast by Kenneth Vandermolen of The Alloy Foundry Company, and were welded together into two piles to avoid a repeat of past history.

In 1989 the cannon itself was refinished compliments of another citizen, John DeLapa. DeLapa, a cannon aficionado, arranged to replace the concrete around the site and to install a gilded information plaque describing the cannon. The refurbished site was dedicated to area citizens by St. Joseph Today and the United States Navy during a ceremony on Flag Day, June 14, 1990.

Contributors to the Cannon Ball Replacement Project:

1. Clare Adkin Family
2. Advance Concepts - John Forney
3. Allegretti Architects
4. Judy, Muriel, Nancy Barkmeier
5. Algird Barvicks
6. Beacon Services Inc.
7. Butzbaugh & Dewane
8. Chester & Priscilla Byrns
9. Clancy's Deli & Gourmet Restaurant
10. Consumers Asphalt - Jack Kinney
11. John DeLapa, Cannon Historian
12. John DeVries Agency Inc.
13. Richard & Phyllis Dowsett
14. Logan Drake, Silver Beach
15. Dumke Family
16. Edgewater Gifts, 315 State Street
17. Duke & Dorothy Ehrenberg
18. Fette, Dumke & Passaro
19. John Florian Family
20. Capt. Robert Gard, U.S. Navy Reserve
21. Gillespie Family, here since 1905
22. Globensky, Gleiss, Bittner & Hyrns
23. G. Daniel & Judy Green
24. Lee B. Granback
25. R.J. Granback

26. Richard O. Grau Family
27. Ruth Gillespie Grootendorst
28. Hammerschmidt Family
29. Enjoy this Park, Hatch Family
30. Judy Herrmann
31. David & Margaret Hills
32. Dale & Marian Hogue
33. Holiday Inn St. Joseph, Mich.
34. Gladys, Bob, Mike, Kendal Holmes
35. Inter-City Bank
36. Stephen's Jewelfire
37. Pete Jorgensen Real Estate
38. Bob, Mary, Carol, Julie & Gary Koch
39. Kara Kotyuk, 1990
40. Kelli A. Kotyuk, 1990
41. Fred & Norma Krause Family
42. Nicholas Lahr
43. Suzanne Lahr
44. Richard Lysaght, Capt. 19 Mi. Inf.
45. Marketing Partners, 1990
46. Kenneth & Bonnie McKeown
47. Patrick & Norine McMullen
48. Rick Miller
49. Steven & Laurie O'Connell
50. Old Kent Bank
51. Don & Marla Owca
52. Peoples State Bank
53. Don Peters Family
54. Mr. & Mrs. A.G. Preston, Jr.
55. Quality Plumbing Company
56. Bob & Karen Rhoa Family
57. Chris, Jeff & Mark Richards
58. B.J. Rimes & Jon J. Rimes
59. William & Margaret Rohn
60. St. Joseph & Benton Harbor Rotary Club, 1989

61. Connie, Dan, Karen & Chris Russell
62. George & Janet Schack
63. Montgomery Shepard Family
64. Signal Travel
65. Franklin & Marguerite Smith
66. Fredda S. Sparks
67. Jack D. Sparks
68. Barbara G. Troost
69. Troost Brothers Furniture, Est. 1903
70. Edward & Thelma Troost
71. Peter Troost
72. David & Linda Upton
73. Frederick S. & Margaret B. Upton
74. Louis C. Upton, Upton Machine Company
75. Henry Vandermolen Family
76. Frank D. & Frank J. Ward, 12th Div.
77. Whitcomb Tower Retirement Center
78. Lyle & Arlene Woodworth
79. Mary Preston Workinger
80. Glenn & Kathryn Zerler
81. Lawrence & Marian Zuhl

Jennifer Schanze in Lake Bluff Park at the site of the restored cannon and cannon balls. May 10, 1991.

Sand Rabbits

Duke Sparks gave us the definition of "sand rabbits."

"First, a 'sand rabbit' can be male or female," Sparks said slowly. His explanation began thoughtfully, gaining momentum as one memory built upon another. "The term is more likely to be associated with males because they bragged more about it. Sand rabbits lived on Pine Street (now Lions Park Drive) and intersecting side streets located below the bluff and west of the tracks. Kids living above the bluff or 'uptown' were called 'town snakes'—a term of endearment when used by a sand rabbit."

Another nickname for those living on top of the bluff, according to Sparks' brother, Tom, was "clay feet," because their homes were built on clay. Both men chuckled at the memory of this childhood rivalry.

Duke Sparks continued, "In the main, sand rabbits came from fine, hard-working German families. The Irish Sparks and a few smaller groups such as the Polish made up the balance. It was amazing how quickly an Irish lad learned to understand an upset mother who was speaking German!

"High school coaches immediately recognized freshman sand rabbits, we lifted our feet higher and ran leaning forward as a result of many years of running in sand."

Their playground extended from the pumping station at the south to the Silver Beach Amusement Park at the north. "Lake Michigan and acres of clean, sandy beach were our backyards," Sparks said. "Our mother once counted sixteen boys' bathing suits hanging in our basement. This was interesting because she had only three sons who were active swimmers at the time. One of the greatest sand rabbit assets was lots of kids in the neighborhood.

"In no time at all, we could organize a posse that included Buck Jones, Tom Mix, Hoot Gibson, Tom Tyler and Ken Maynard. Even Hollywood could not put this group together. No battle in the sand hills ever included less than a thousand hostile Indians. A reenactment of a World War I battle would have taken the WPA three days to fill in the trenches that were dug in the sand.

"It was a German tradition for mothers to bake on Saturday. I feel a sadness for anyone who did not have the opportunity to walk the full length of Pine Street and smell the fantastic aroma of freshly baked coffee cake and bread. It was a ritual for Sparks' kids to visit the homes of at least three sand rabbits on Saturday mornings.

"Anytime two or more senior citizen 'sand rabbits' get together and reminisce, they usually end up expressing this thought: growing up as a sand rabbit was the greatest, happiest life a kid could possibly enjoy. It never occured to us that we were economically poorer than church mice.

"I cannot relate to the current generation of sand rabbits, if they truly exist. Possibly, being a sand rabbit was dependent on more than a place of residence. It may have been a way of life that is now gone forever."

Utah and Earl E. Sparks moved to 1102 Pine Street in St. Joseph in 1926. They had seven sons, Daniel, Tom, Charles "Shorty," Earl "Duke," Jack, Alan and James.

A Bomb Shelter on Ridgeway

Cliff Emlong recalls a period beginning with World War II and including the atomic bomb threat that changed everyone's life. Locally, groups were set up to organize neighborhoods in case of attack. Dave Mather was the city organizer of these groups which held their meetings at the former St. Joseph Senior High School on Niles Avenue (now Milton Park).

In the Edgewater area, Cliff Emlong served as the warden, Ralph Newland provided encouragement as his assistant, Al Gast was appointed block captain and their messenger was young Walt Wolf, Jr. After the regularly scheduled meetings the older members of this group retired to the Brass Rail to plan their strategy for the coming week.

"We really worked on Walt Wolf," said Emlong. "Ask him about it."

Wolf laughed at the memory. "They had me riding my bicycle around town at all hours of the day and night," he said. "We had blackouts and had to plan for the event of air raids in the dark of night."

With Sputnik and powerful Russia staring America in the face, it was decided that an air raid shelter be built for Edgewater. A site was selected on Ridgeway and detailed plans were made for the design, rations and equipment for the shelter.

However, when the group got down to who would be eligible to use the shelter, the arguments began. For a period of about three months, the meetings became controversial and loud as family members and relatives were discussed and accepted or rejected for protection inside the proposed shelter.

Finally, Cliff Emlong and Bob Upton along with a few others came to the conclusion that the neighbors would never agree on who could use the shelter and the project was canceled (which likely saved the neighborhood from destruction as well).

* * *

Emlong also tells of the recurring "Battle of Ridgeway" over whether to maintain the beautiful brick street or pave it over with blacktop. Sometime in the 1950s, when Mayor Waldo Tiscornia was up for reelection as St. Joseph City Commissioner, the battle turned political. Emlong and Larry Bell took the mayor's side to pave the street and found themselves blacklisted from neighborhood meetings regarding the issue. Pegge Emlong was ready to disown her husband who, along with Bell, stood alone against the neighbors and against the cherished bricks.

At the end of that phase, Tiscornia won the election but lost the battle of the bricks and everyone became friendly again. Within a few years, Emlong was elected to the city commission and later became the mayor.

In 1961, St. Joseph supporter Pat McMullen brought the issue of paving Ridgeway back to Tiscornia's attention. Tiscornia responded with a letter, part of which is recorded here:

"Now, the pointed needle that you have stuck into the most fleshy part of my body regarding the paving of Ridgeway, which I had entirely forgotten about until you deliberately needled my ego into emotional upsets back to some years ago. My only rebuttal to your needle is that you get on our good, mutual friend, Commissioner Cliff Emlong, and write him no end to deliver the down-trodden, poor residents from the swamps, mud and rain holes even though a nice, smooth pavement might destroy the Old England atmosphere that the present beautiful brick pavement now gives them."

Clifford R. Emlong *has lived on Ridgeway for 55 years. He is the owner of Emlong's Nursery. He has served on the Community Chest (now Blossomland United Way), and on the Berrien County Board of Public Works in addition to his service as a St. Joseph city commissioner from 1958-1965 and as mayor from 1962-1965. Waldo Tiscornia was a commissioner from 1938-1955 and served as mayor from 1942-1955.*

St. Joseph Memories

Today, Ardys Schultz enjoys walking as a form of exercise. When she was a teenager living on Lewis Avenue, a favorite Sunday afternoon pastime was walking to downtown St. Joseph with a group of friends to listen to a band concert or just to see who was home from the service. Sometimes the group would walk to Benton Harbor and back, but they had to get home in time to get ready to go to Shadowland Ballroom to dance the night away. In the 1940s young people often went to Crystal Palace on Saturday nights and to Shadowland on Sunday evenings.

Young Ardys Schultz (then Ludwig) did not drive and neither did most of her friends. The ones who did were allowed to use the family car "on occasion." Drivers Education was unheard of in those days. Schultz remembers

how she received her first driver's license. A friend was going to teach her how to drive, so she went to the police station to get a permit. She told the woman there that she wanted an application for a driver's license and before she knew what happened, she had the license. The woman never asked if she could drive.

Other fond memories are eating the wonderful hot fudge sundaes at Gillespie's Drug Store, going to the Caldwell Theater (on the east side of the 400 block of State Street) for a movie and then walking across the street to Mawhinney's for a burger and dancing in the back room.

* * *

Before Lewis Avenue, the Ludwig family homestead was a farm in Twelve Corners. During winter months, father and son, Max and Franklin "Duke" Ludwig, and several neighbors would trek over to the Paw Paw River with chain saws and cut blocks of ice to fit the families' ice-boxes. These blocks were stored in a specially constructed icehouse and covered with sawdust for insulation.

The ice would last well into summer, and when it was gone the families in Twelve Corners relied upon deliveries from the iceman several times a week to keep their ice-boxes cold. The iceboxes themselves had large pans underneath which needed to be emptied on a daily basis as the ice melted. If anyone wanted ice for a drink, that person had to chip bits away from the block with an ice pick (a tool like a sharpened screwdriver).

Ardys J. Schultz has lived in the area all her life. She was born in Twelve Corners, moved to St. Joseph as a young girl, and married Louis C. Schultz in 1947. They raised four children—Kathy, Karen, Gary, David— in Benton Harbor and on Paw Paw Lake in Coloma.

The Christmas Tree House

The Schlenzka family home at 823 State Street in St. Joseph has been known to some as the "Christmas Tree House." "I don't know the reason," said Dr. Paula M. Schlenzka, whose parents, Dr. and Mrs. Paul and Ethel Schlenzka moved into the house in 1947. "However, from 1947 to 1984, the red brick on the bottom was painted red, and the shingles on the second and third floors were painted green with white and black trim around the windows."

Dr. Paul Schlenzka's chiropractic office was on the first floor of the house, and the family resided in the upper floors until his death in 1966. Ethel Schlenzka passed away in 1980, leaving the house to her daughter.

Paula Schlenzka followed in her father's footsteps as a chiropractic physician but chose to return the first floor to living quarters and locate her office elsewhere. "The Old St. Joseph Neighborhood Preservation Association (OSJNPA) has done a lot for the area," said Schlenzka, a past president of the group whose boundries run south of downtown St. Joseph from Lake Boulevard to Main Street. "I decided to keep the family home as my home in our lovely, historic neighborhood."

Schlenzka's house is on record with the organization as being one of the best examples of Queen Anne style shingles—diamond and teardrop shapes—in the area. Her wicker front porch swing dates from about the time the house was built circa 1904 and is the only one of its kind locally.

Schlenzka has a copy of the original title to the property which starts with Benjamin Hoyt's addition to St. Joseph on June 23, 1874. On the abstract of the title there is a warranty deed dated November 25, 1902, and a mortgage dated November 1, 1907.

Dr. Paula M. Schlenzka has lived in this house all of her life. Her practice is currently located at 812-A Ship Street.

Living in St. Joseph

Note: *Following are excerpts from Gladys Eisenhart-Brown's book* When I Lived on Lake Shore Drive and Other Stories.

When I was eleven years old, we lived upstairs above Burkhard Brother's General Store which was across the street from the Hotel Whitcomb. I used to watch the women in deck chairs along the sidewalk holding mirrors under their chins to enhance their tans. Years later, when I saw Radar O'Riley doing this on the television series M.A.S.H., it reminded me of the Whitcomb ladies.

* * *

Polly the parrot was very popular with Whitcomb guests, but unfortunately her vocabulary belonged on the waterfront.

* * *

When I was in high school, I worked for the Grace B. Pauley Company at 406 State Street. Mrs. Pauley used to call on me to try on junior size dresses that she was considering buying for the store.

One day, a salesman brought in a new line, but she didn't like the flat lines across the bust, and she told him so. He replied that this was 1950 and the "new look" was to flatten the bust. She promptly informed him that it had taken her years to get her bust to stand up, and she would be damned if she would flatten it out.

* * *

Soon after my high-school graduation in 1950, I went to work at Iaggi's Jewelry Store in St. Joseph. I was asked to sign an agreement stating that I would not quit for at least one year due to the extensive training involved with learning to recognize the many china, crystal and silver patterns carried in the store.

The job was short-lived when, after only a few months of employment, I was told that the store had been sold. However, the training remained firmly in my memory, and over the years when I dined in people's homes I often didn't recognize what I was eating, but I always knew the names of their tableware patterns.

*   *   *

What started out as a "get-rich-quick" job in 1951 lasted sixteen years. I originally intended to work at Holly's Grill long enough to buy a new Easter outfit and maybe stay the summer and add to my trousseau.

John Hallberg hired me as a "Holly Dolly" as their waitresses were called. The money was good...the people were nice...and I stayed seven years at the northeast corner of Main and Pleasant Streets with a few months off to have three babies. I kid my children that three out of the four worked at Holly's before they were born.

Main Street at that time was part of the highway between Chicago and Detroit and we served "all kinds" of customers. Holly's was open until midnight every night, there was no air conditioning, and the jukebox played constantly. It cost five cents or five plays for a quarter to fill the smoky air with strains of "The Tennessee Waltz,"

"Across the Alley from the Alamo," "Beautiful, Beautiful, Brown Eyes," and "In the Cool, Cool, Cool of the Evening."

I remember waiting on many nice families through the years. Some of the regulars were the Hallbergs, the Filstrups, the Newlands, the Taylors with their young son Ronald, the Zollars, the Hogues, and everyday there would be a Gillespie or two or three or four.

Gladys Eisenhart later worked in Holly's Heath Company cafeteria for nine years.

Eleanor Roosevelt at the
Economic Club of Southwestern Michigan

The Economic Club has been meeting since 1943 in south-western Michigan. Past presidents were Louis Upton, 1943-1953, and John Paul Taylor, 1953-1983; current president is Michael K. Cook. The first speaker roster for the 1943-1944 season included Paul A. Hoffman, Dr. Gerald Wendt, Dr. Leo Wolman, Dr. Margaret Mead, Dr. Victor G. Heiser and Eric A. Johnston.

Priscilla Upton Byrns remembers neighbors and friends telling about the evening that Eleanor Roosevelt was slated to appear. During the program years of 1953-1954—when Roosevelt was scheduled to speak—the club was for men only. They met in the Tropical Room at the Whitcomb Hotel for dinner and the speaker.

Many local women wanted to hear her address, but due to the club's exclusive male membership, women were not allowed. This regulation, however, did not stop some enterprising local women.

They conspired with Leon Harris, manager of the Whitcomb, who fitted them with waitress uniforms. After they helped the regular waitresses serve dinner, the women stood in the back of the room to hear Roosevelt. Members of the head table, who recognized the "wait-resses," were in stitches.

Among the "waitresses" were Dorothy Vawter, Beth Upton, Helen Grootendorst, Phyllis Preston, Daisy Hoffmann and Katherine "Kit" Campbell.

The Economic Club meets today at Lake Michigan College's Community Center, recently renamed the Mendel Center. For nearly half a century, the club has brought to our community knowledgeable and notable people who influence world events.

Priscilla Upton Byrns is the daughter of Frederick S. and Margaret B. Upton. She is married to Chester Byrns, a retired Berrien County circuit court judge.

Honesty is the Best Policy

Even at the age of 89, John Kowalski discovered that there are still lessons left to be learned. "I'm not going to carry that much money around again, that's a cinch," Kowalski said after losing his wallet containing $685 and getting it back again in downtown St. Joseph.

Under normal circumstances, Kowalski carried a minimal amount of money. But on this day in 1955, he had cashed a check intending to purchase a heating unit. With the money in his pocket, he strolled downtown from his home on Lewis Avenue to pay his monthly utility bills. He paid his electric bill at Indiana and Michigan's office at 409 State Street, but arrived at the Michigan Gas Utilities Company at 204 State without his wallet.

After a few moments of searching, Kowalski returned home thinking the money was gone forever and wondering how he could do without the heating unit. He contacted his daughter, Mrs. Eugene (Katherine) Schreiber who lived next door, and explained the loss to her.

In the meantime, Mrs. George Rybarcyzk had picked up the wallet which she found lying on the sidewalk in front of Troost Brothers at 403 State. Kowalski's identification enabled her to return his wallet with the money intact. A $5 reward went with the return.

John V. Kowalski was born in Poland in 1865. He lived in St. Joseph from 1883 until he passed away in 1963 at the age of 97. This story was submitted by his great-grandson, Kenneth John Leonarduzzi, and a granddaughter, Mrs. Felix (Margaret Schreiber) Leonarduzzi of Iron River, Michigan, formerly of St. Joseph.

You Can't Make Me!

William Ast remembers one Saturday in May when he and his wife, Mildred, took their son, Rick, to the Blossom Parade in St. Joseph.

After the parade, they cut across Market Street on the way to the car. As they reached the tree lawn, little Rick looked up and saw the dentist's office.

He threw himself down and started kicking and shouting, "I'm not going in there! You can't make me go in there!"

Just then, Dr. Clell K. Johnson came back to work. The shocked dentist stood watching Rick in disbelief, shaking his head and repeating, "I can't be that bad. I can't be that bad."

William Ast has lived in the area all of his life. He retired in 1975 from the Whirlpool Corporation. William "Rick" Ast III is the assistant metro editor at the Herald-Palladium.

William "Rick" Ast III

Benton Harbor
by Emery George

How often I have staged a funeral
of years as far away as the town will cake
in summer dust; extra-wide Main Street, fake
store fronts, car dealers, phenomenal

Sundays of bad music; garage, trash to take
to the curb. Coal cellars fill with ephemeral
smiles: a school dance. We hear oracular
cries of seagulls over a summer lake.

Now these days I hear no seagulls cry
for people I once loved. I bury them
in mounds of maple leaves and thoughts as dry,

and will now try a different stratagem:
the pale blue of a February sky,
the soft bronze of a baroque requiem.

*This poem is reprinted by permission of **Dr. Emery George**. He is the
author of several books including* A Gift of Nerve: Poems 1966-1977
*(Ann Arbor: Kylix Press, 1978) where this poem first appeared.
George received the Avery and Jule Hopwood award in poetry from the
University of Michigan in 1960 among other honors for his work. He
currently resides in Princeton, New Jersey.*

When I Grow Up, I Want to be Mayor

Phyllis Thurkettle tells a story about Frank Smith visiting her third grade classroom at Lincoln Elementary in the St. Joseph Public School system. She vividly recalls Smith sitting at the head of the classroom in one of the little third grade chairs with his knees nearly to his shoulders. The children sat on the floor at his feet.

As part of the social studies curriculum, Smith had been invited to tell about his job as a leader of the community. He explained the commission type of government in St. Joseph, and that he was selected by members of the commission to be mayor. One brave child raised his hand and asked, "Mr. Smith, why did you want to become mayor?"

Smith told the children, "When I was a little boy we lived off of Hilltop Road. I used to walk up and down that road, which was mostly fields and farmland. It was then that I decided I wanted to be mayor of St. Joseph someday. And I made it."

He finished by encouraging the children to ask him anything else about being a mayor. According to Thurkettle, they all looked up in awe at the big man in the little chair and were silent for a while before anyone else uttered a word.

When Smith stood up to leave, the children's eyes traveled up his tall frame. There was no doubt in anyone's mind that this man was the mayor.

Phyllis Thurkettle taught school for 33 1/2 years. She has lived in this area since 1957, and is a native of Grand Rapids.

Franklin H. Smith served on the St. Joseph City Commission from 1967 to 1991. He was mayor from 1972 to 1991.

A Place at the Blossom Parade

Brad Laughlin shares one of his earliest, strongest and most lasting impressions of St. Joseph and Benton Harbor—the local custom of staking claims to viewing spots on the Blossom Parade route by leaving lawn chairs or blankets at curbside on the day before the parade and having people respect the claim. Laughlin assures us that in his native Detroit the chairs and blankets would have disappeared overnight!

After nearly five years of witnessing this tradition, he still says, "Incredible! People here leave equipment and toys unattended on their lawns and their cars running while they dash into shops. Moreover, local house-holders pay scant attention to locking their doors. What serenity! I sound like a walking chamber of commerce but there are few places left like this."

Lee Passaro arranges her chair the day before the 1991 Blossom Parade.

* * *

Laughlin's story brings to mind a similar tale told to New York audiences by comedian Lew Schneider. Schneider says his car was broken into shortly after he moved to New York from Chicago. He told the police, "I've been here 28 days. What the hell's going on?"

The New York police replied, "Look, they got a lot of cars to break into, and they get to them as fast as they can."

* * *

In Detroit, Laughlin left his home for a scant half-hour and returned to find the place ransacked. Thinking the perpetrators might still be on the premises, he dialed 911, explained the circumstances and waited outside for the police. It took the police more than an hour to arrive. Another time, when a woman was mugged in front of his home, Laughlin helped her inside, and again called 911. This time the response time was one hour and forty-five minutes.

He compares these incidents with one that happened to a friend of his who was a patient at Mercy Memorial Medical Center. The friend was in immediate need of a bed pan and couldn't reach the intercom call button. However, he could reach the telephone, so he dialed 911. Within minutes, a nurse was at his side with the necessary equipment and the moment was saved.

Bradford Laughlin is a retired patent attorney who has lived in St. Joseph since he married Kathy Kemp five years ago. He recently noticed that the front door to his house was unlocked and had very likely been that way for several days. He seldom locks his car doors anymore. Laughlin wonders if he is "going native" under the gentle influence of his friends and neighbors?

*   *   *

Marilyn Peterson tells another story related to our community services. In the summer of 1986, Peterson's daughter, Monica, was hit by a car while she was riding a bicycle at the corner of Hilltop and Niles Road during the noon hour. The St. Joseph police heard of the accident as they passed by Judge David M. Peterson who was doing his daily jog. The police raced Peterson to the hospital to meet his daughter who luckily only suffered minor injuries.

Marilyn and David Peterson *were raised in Lawton and moved to St. Joseph in 1970 when he was hired by a local law firm. She works in tourism and education.*

Continuity

Tom and Elenore Lyons retired in 1984. For the next five years, they traveled throughout the United States in motor homes, making several cross country treks to the Benton Harbor-St. Joseph area to visit friends and relatives. Experimenting with various R.V. Parks, they settled on the House of David Park which was quiet and close to everyone they knew. They found the manager, Dale Smith, to be a very courteous and gentle man. And Tom especially drew satisfaction from being on the former site of the famous House of David baseball park, a natural amphitheater to the House of David amusement park.

On one of these trips, sometime in the late 1980s, Tom asked Smith about Barney Dalager who played on the St. Joseph Merchants baseball team in the late 1940s. Lloyd "Barney" Dalager was a House of David member who played with the Merchants after the colony's team became only a traveling club. Dalager was an electrician for the House of David and couldn't be spared from his duties to travel full time with the team.

He had been a member of the famous House of David "Pepper Squad," a group of four or five men who did tricks with baseballs that not even the Harlem Globe Trotters did with basketballs. Lyons remembered Dalager as a short, compact young man with a full, auburn beard and long hair in a queue as required by the House of David. He told Smith, "Barney had the best disposition anybody could have, a smile on his face and a twinkle in his eyes. He was a good hitter and a tremendous fielder at third base, shortstop or second base."

As Lyons repeated that Dalager had been an electrician with the House of David, Smith exclaimed, "He still is! There he goes right now!" Lo and behold, bouncing past the office was a pick-up truck driven by a compact man with a full white beard and hair in a queue.

Barney Dalager is still a member of the House of David and gives his permission to use this story since it isn't "too derogatory." Lyons promises to catch up with him on another visit and talk over old baseball stories.

Tom Dewhirst adds to this story. For many years the traveling team had to contend with dirt roads that were poorly signed. As team manager during the 1930s, Dewhirst remembers frequent stops at gas stations to ask for directions.

On one occasion, Dalager was the lead driver and he missed a turn. When the second driver finally caught up with him and told him he'd missed the turn, Dalager jumped out of his car. Looking up at the sky, he shouted, "Where's the dipper? Where's the dipper?"

The Decoration People

Most St. Joseph residents are familiar with the flat-roofed house on the corner of Wallace and Wilson that is almost always decorated for holidays, school sporting events, graduations, family celebrations and any other conceivable reason. The house belongs to Richard and Phyllis Dowsett. She says, "To say we have fun with decorating is an understatement. It all started with my parents who made and displayed holiday decorations as I was growing up. We've gotten addicted to the habit."

They have received many notes and phone calls from people who enjoy their seasonal scenes. Families stop by for picture-taking sessions; one little girl donated her own teddy bear to a St. Joseph High School display; and on one memorable Christmas Eve, Santa and Mrs. Claus dropped in unannounced to express their admiration.

One Halloween they decided to use lots of pumpkins in the yard. Since their home is located across the street from St. Joseph High School, they expected some of their pumpkins to disappear—even though the students usually behaved respectfully toward their displays. When the pumpkins disappeared faster than they liked, the Dowsetts decided to take steps to eliminate the problem.

They sprinkled garlic into Vick's vapor salve and smeared this mixture generously onto the bottoms of the pumpkins. Later that evening, they became suspicious when they heard a car idling outside. Peering out the window, they saw a young woman sitting in the passenger seat of a yellow Volkswagon, and a young man selecting a pumpkin and delivering it to the lap of the girl in the car.

As the boy returned to the yard for another pumpkin, Dick ran outside with a camera and snapped a picture of the boy placing another stinky pumpkin in the girl's lap. The stunned young man waited until his eyesight recovered from the flash and drove off quickly down the street. Word must have spread quickly around the high school, because the Dowsetts didn't lose another pumpkin after that.

The Dowsett House

Another time, when Phyllis' sons Keene and Timothy Taylor played football for St. Joseph High School, she found it challenging to decorate for Halloween and support the team at the same time. The solution for Phyllis was to "bury" St. Joseph's football opponents and place tombstones with the scores over their "graves."

One evening Phyllis received a telephone call from a woman in Stevensville, who asked, "Are you missing something?"

Phyllis replied that she wasn't sure.

Seems as though Phyllis' fame had traveled to Stevensville, because when a tombstone was deposited in the other woman's yard, she knew who to call to come and retrieve it.

On another very warm Halloween evening, Phyllis and Dick decided to replace two of their artificial ghosts which were sitting in lawn chairs with the real things—themselves dressed as ghosts. It was a beautiful evening and the Dowsetts sat very still listening to comments the passerbys made about the people who live in this house. The trick or treaters were really surprised when their treats were handed to them from the "real ghosts" in the lawn chairs.

Phyllis Dowsett carries her enthusiasm to her work as the executive director of the Southwestern Michigan Tourist Council. She formerly held the position of director of Blossomtime, Inc. and is a lifetime supporter of the area.

P.J. "Pat" Mcmullen, the Mayor of Irish Hills

In 1984, Pat McMullen walked into St. Joseph Today's upstairs office at 520 Pleasant Street and plunked a tiny bottle of whiskey on the desk. He said, "Here, you're going to need this."

As the new director of St. Joseph Today, I thanked him and put the airplane-size bottle into the refrigerator. Through the years, seeing that bottle—with the label "Pat McMullen, Mayor of Irish Hills, St. Joseph, Mich."—and remembering his support gave me many comfortable moments.

Six years later, a short time after *On the Banks of the Ole St. Joe* was printed, McMullen paid another visit to St. Joseph Today. This time he arrived bearing a small box containing six miniature bottles of the brew. He said, "Here, you deserve this." Thank you again, Pat!

The personalized whiskey is an extension of McMullen's miniature bottle collection which currently exceeds 25,000. In addition to his private label, McMullen has drawers full of reserve stock which he calls "trading stock." These are duplicates of the masses of bottles which line the basement in the St. Joseph home he shares with his wife Norine.

"For every bottle I've collected, someone else gave me one or I traded one," says McMullen of the alphabetized collection which resides impressively behind glass cases constructed especially for the tiny bottles. "It's been a lifetime of friendship with other collectors."

There are gins, rums, vodkas, scotches, whiskeys, cordials and wine in the collection of bottles that are designed in various shapes such as round, square, flat, pyramid or teardrop. Some of the glass bottles are made to resemble fiddles, animals, sports equipment, houses and people. Others are ceramic figurines in the form of birds, fish, soldiers, guns, chessmen and more. The manufacturers of Delft china make blue and white replicas of windmills and Dutch homes. Their miniature bottles are served in the first class section of KLM airlines.

Part of his collection includes a set of "boxer bottles." Joe Louis' label on Kentucky Straight Bourbon Whiskey reads "Champion of Them All" and was bottled by the Joe Louis Distilling Company of Lawrenceburg, Kentucky. Jack Dempsey has two labels on blended whiskey. One is 86.8 proof bottled by the Jack Dempsey Company of Dundalk, Maryland and the other is 90 proof bottled by McKesson & Robbins of Aladdin, Pennsylvania. Both whiskeys were blended to Dempsey's specifications. Finally, there are two John L. [Sullivan] brands: 90 proof Straight Bourbon Whiskey and 90 proof Straight Rye Whiskey.

McMullen has 18 "fiddle bottles" which were created by the Bardstown Distillery of Bardstown, Kentucky in honor of Stephen Foster who immortalized the South with folk songs such as "My Old Kentucky Home," "Old Folks at Home," "Massa's in De Cold, Cold Ground," "Old Black Joe," "Beautiful Dreamer," "Old Susanna" and "Jeanie with the Light Brown Hair."

The brown glass bottles, shaped like violins, are five inches tall and two inches wide. The proofs vary from 86 to 100 percent and are named "Old Anthem," "Old Bard," "Old Fiddle," "Bard's Town," "Bard's Town Bond" and "Bourbon Springs."

One of the bottles, Bard's Town 100 proof, was made in 1934 and bottled in 1938. A miniature fiddle-shaped book containing many of Stephen Foster's folk songs accompanied the bottle.

McMullen notes that, "all of my 'fiddles' are in perfect tune!"

Miniature bottles, called "nips," contain between one and six-tenths to two ounces of liquor. Most of McMullen's collection is sealed, and about 95% of it is in mint condition, but the contents evaporate over time. He tries to counteract the evaporation by double sealing his bottles with wax.

The first miniatures were sealed with corks and called "corkers." Then came screw tops and tear tops (like pop-top cans). Glass miniatures, like corks, are becoming a thing of the past, being replaced by plastic.

McMullen started his collection in 1933 when he was given a bottle shaped like a dollhouse. He filled the bottle with colored water and passed it on to his daughter. He started noticing the bottles on trains and brought dining car decanters home from his travels.

In the beginning he collected everything, but now specializes in whiskey. Approximately 15,000 whiskey bottles are on display. He has them categorized into bourbons, blends, ryes and scotches, all alphabetized within their types.

Miniatures date back to the late 1800s, but mass production began in the 1930s, halted during Prohibition, then resumed. Until the mid-1970s, the bottles were only available on airplanes or trains and were intended as samples not to be sold.

Pat McMullen is retired from Theisen-Clemens Oil Company. His Irish green business card reads "When the urge comes to exercise, I lie down until it passes by." He wears kelly green ties in honor of his ancestry and says his home on St. Joseph Drive is the "closest thing to being in Ireland."

One Little, Two Little...Six Little Christmas Trees

Marilyn Pape creates Christmas trees. Her sixth one came into being when she wanted to decorate the Fort Miami Heritage Society headquarters, where she serves as executive secretary. Pape made a table tree with handmade lace and satin ornaments in Victorian style. Under this tree are small Victorian figures on one side and dated Santas on the other.

She owns her grandfather's collection of cigar bands prior to 1918 and also collects stamps depicting our country's history, Nancy Ann storybook and other dolls, mice, nativity scenes and memorabilia from *The Wizard of Oz*. Some of these collections work nicely with the trees which crowd the house in Benton Harbor that Pape shares with her father, William Pape.

Her *Wizard of Oz* tree in the den is hung with little Dorothys, Tin Men, Scarecrows and Cowardly Lions. Pape fashioned a rainbow with a fluffy cloud for the top and constructed a version of the Emerald City to round out the room.

The heirloom tree owns a special place in the family living room. It has baskets crocheted by her grandmother, Emma Pape Elliott, who died in 1948; glass ornaments her father and mother (the late Marian Pape) collected when they married in 1930; family photographs in homemade frames; and three angels symbolizing Marilyn and her two sisters. Part of Marilyn's mice collection—mostly gifts from her sisters—hangs on this tree.

The kitchen tree features miniature cereal boxes, utensils, canned foods and vegetables. At its base are miniature appliances which actually work.

A table tree in the bathroom is covered with seashells, coral and seahorses Pape inherited from an aunt. In the dining room is the largest tree in the collection. Many ornaments on this tree were handmade by Pape and her mother. "She was a skilled craftsperson and I inherited some of her talent," Pape said. The matchboxes, medicine bottles and egg shells they decorated with paint, ribbons and sequins testify to their creativity.

Their are other ornaments on this tree from Pape's trip to Germany and underneath is a fence constructed in 1937 by her father. "I wanted a fence like my Aunt Ruth's," said Pape. "So he stayed up at night after we went to bed and made it. It was a very special surprise."

In addition to the trees and nativity scenes, Pape says, "I also display two dollhouses that are nearly 50 years old and are from my childhood—my first one that is—and two old sleds. One sled is decorated with a large bow, and the other sits in front of the fireplace with a pile of stuffed animals. The leader is 'Al' a Malemute pup purchased in Alaska."

"If there is anything better than to be loved it is loving."

Anonymous

IV. Loving

At the Bend of the Old St. Joe
words & music by Rex L. Buell
published by the Wilbur Templin Music Company

There's a dear old river flowing,
Through a valley far away
Where the setting sun's last glowing,
On the golden ripples lay;
When the twilight shadows gather,
And the songbirds go to rest,
Steals a picture of a valley,
And a river I love best.
I hear the church bells ringing,
As they did in days of yore,
The song my mother's singing,
Steals from out the kitchen door;
Where the morning glories twining,
Comes a scent of new mown hay,
In the evening breeze soft sighing,
I dream I hear you say...

Chorus...
Meet me at the bend of the Old Saint Joe,
Where you and I met long ago;
Where as children we played,
'Neath the wide spreading shade,
Of willows where violets grow.
Bright moon shines down with a gentle glow,
On the waters that peacefully flow,
There with my canoe,
I'll be waiting for you,
At the bend of the Old Saint Joe.

When the moon is softly beaming,
Down upon the Old Saint Joe.
Where its silver ripples gleaming,
There the water lilies grow;
It is then I love to wander,
There beside the dear old stream,
Of fond recollections ponder,
And of childhood days I dream.
Remember how we used to swing,
In the grapevine on the hill,
And how we waded in the spring,
That ran down to the mill;
When the clinking wheels are turning,
As we used to watch them then,
In the sound of waters churning,
I hear you say again...

Chorus...

*This song was submitted by **Joe Bartz and Virginia Handy** from the collection of Mary Handy. It is reprinted by permission of Templin's Music and Electronics of Elkhart, Indiana. Wilbur Templin purchased the business in 1905 and named it the Wilbur Templin Music Company. Rex L. Buell worked for the company and, like Templin, was an accomplished pianist. After Buell composed the song in 1907, Templin paid for its printing, thus becoming its publisher and chief purveyor.*

When Elkhart celebrated its centennial in 1958, Templin's wife Elsie had the song reprinted as a give-away item for the store. The music is still available through Templin's Music and Electronics, 3420 S. Main Street, Elkhart, Indiana 46517, (219) 293-0343.

A Helping Hand

Amey Upton tells a story relayed to her by Hank and Joanne Kasischke about her late grandmother-in-law, Margaret Upton, who commissioned embroidery pieces during the Great Depression from people who were unable to find work. Professing a household need for the pieces, Mrs. Upton purchased the handiwork in order to provide financial support during difficult times for talented, hard-working local people. Many of the pieces of hand-embroidered linen are still being used by Margaret Upton's grandchildren today.

Amey Upton is married to U.S. Congressman Fred Upton who is the grandson of the late Frederick S. and Margaret B. Upton. Hank and Joanne Kasischke own The Downtown Printer at 512 Broad Street in downtown St. Joseph.

Margaret Upton

243

A Lucky New Year's Eve

In the 1930s, Tom Lyons was dating Betty Reep, a cute, tiny girl with a little voice who reminded him of "Betty Boop." They weren't serious, but both loved to dance and dated for that purpose.

When the clock struck midnight one New Year's Eve at Shadowland Ballroom, Lyons kissed Reep according to the custom. They were standing next to Eddie Demchinski, a friend of both of them. Demchinski turned to Reep and gave her a hearty smack, leaving Lyons staring at his date, a beautiful blonde.

Elenore and Tom Lyons

Lyons tentatively said, "Guess we'd better kiss for New Year's Eve also."

She smiled and agreed. Afterward, she and Demchinski danced away before Lyons could get her name.

That kiss had Lyons shook up! He couldn't get the kiss or the girl out of his mind.

A few weeks later, Lyons saw the blonde girl standing near one of the large stoves which were scattered throughout Shadowland. He approached her and asked, "Aren't you the girl I kissed on New Year's Eve?"

Elenore Lockwitz smiled sweetly and nodded yes.

He asked her to dance, and again she said yes.

That was the beginning of a marriage that marked 53 years on July 31, 1991. The Lyons had five children, Marcia, Peggy, Tom, Teddy and Kurt.

Rocky Gap Park

A very popular "Lovers Lane" spot for Twin Cities' young people was Rocky Gap Park before the road was narrowed to make way for landscaping improvements (including expanded parking facilities and a stairway to Lake Michigan).

In the late 1930s, Tom Lyons and Elenore Lockwitz were "steadies." They had seen a movie at the Liberty Theater in downtown Benton Harbor and headed straight for Rocky Gap.

Tom was driving his parents' gun-metal gray 1937 Ford V-8. There had been quite a bit of rain, and as he pulled off the road, he spotted a mud hole between the edge of the bluff and the road. He attempted to navigate the car around the hole, but the driver's side sank into it, and the car was suddenly slanting at a precarious angle.

Tom tried rocking the car. Then he climbed out and pushed. Elenore also tried rocking the car, but she kept killing the engine.

They changed places. He revved up the engine and with his foot digging the pedal into the floorboard and then wildly hitting the brake, he succeeded in getting the car to rock. However, unknown to Tom, as he was rocking the car Elenore was leaning against it trying to push it out. Suddenly, the car shot out of the mud hole leaving the surprised Elenore hanging at a 45-degree angle over the puddle. Down she went, falling smack into the middle of the giant mud hole.

Tom backed up and grimaced when he saw poor Elenore standing there pathetically covered with mud. She was wearing a new fall coat that she had just made in home economics class at school. As they drove to the Lockwitz home, Elenore decided she would have to "come clean" with the truth. Like George Washington, she was reluctant to tell a lie. Leaving out the details of how and where she fell, Elenore simply told her mother that she had fallen into a very deep mud puddle.

Tom Lyons proposed to Elenore Lockwitz at the Liberty Theater in 1938 during a showing of A Yank at Oxford. *They later confessed the whole story to Mrs. Lockwitz who laughed and told them that she knew all about Lovers Lanes and they could have told her the whole story in the first place.*

Rocky Gap Bluff

(Benton Harbor, 1977)
by Gary E. McCormick

The hungry lake chews the bluffs
bit by chomping bit
spitting chunks into the wild wash

The birch holds its ground
with skin peeled roots
grabbing with white knuckle grip

A boulder breaks loose
scrambles freewheeling
cartwheeling from glacial bonds

Thoughts in a Maternity Ward
by Gary E. McCormick

A stubborn chunk of chalk
harbors in tree shade
as a crocus grunts forth
birthing headfirst to daylight

In this context I watch
your pink wrinkles blossom
your blue eyes bloom
born this blessed spring day

Lake Michigan Sunset
by Gary E. McCormick

The bright orange ball of sun
cut in half by the horizon
ducks deep beneath the great lake
holds its breath and swims slowly
surfaces at daybreak behind the loungers
sitting in the sunwatch bleachers
high on the lake's great bluffs.

They are wonderstruck lovers
of the rising and setting sun.

Cliche'
by **Gary E. McCormick**

"You're pretty as a picture."
Nothing hackneyed about that.

She was plain, never heard
such words before in her context.

What she heard was as fresh
as the rose tucked beneath
the pillow of her beautiful dream.

Gary E. McCormick is an advertising representative for the Herald-Palladium. *His first book of poetry,* One of the Mamy Roses, *will be published this year.*

A Wedding at the Policemen's Ball

Elsie Kesterke Kolberg fondly remembers February 22, 1936. On that day, she was married to Roy Hallman at the Policemen's Ball.

Here's how it happened. Elsie and Roy had been dating for about a year. She worked at G.C. Murphy Co. as a clerk at the candy counter and all the policemen used to stop for samples of candy.

One evening, when Roy was leaving the apartment on State Street which Elsie shared with her sister, he was stopped by a St. Joseph policeman for a faulty headlight. The two started talking and the officer suggested that Elsie and Roy get married and have the ceremony at the Policemen's Ball.

This idea must have held great appeal for Roy since the next evening he proposed to Elsie.

The proceeds from the ball and the public wedding benefited the St. Joseph Police Department. The $500 which was raised purchased new uniforms for the officers. State police were called in to guard the city while the St. Joseph Police handled the staging of the wedding held in the Shadowland Ballroom at Silver Beach.

The ceremony began with Fred Stueland singing "I Love You Truly" and approximately 1,500 people witnessed the Reverend J. Arthur Palm of Saron Lutheran Church as he read the service over an amplifying system.

The bride was dressed by Catheryne Shepard, owner of a very exclusive dress shop in downtown St. Joseph named

Shepard & Benning. The young couple was generously showered with $400 worth of wedding gifts from St. Joseph merchants.

It was truly a memorable evening for the newly married Hallmans and a great benefit to the policemen's fund raising efforts.

A Day at the Blossom Parade
(and what it can lead to)

In the early 1940s, Lyle C. Witte was invited to attend the annual Grand Floral Parade as the guest of Carl Schuett and his mother, Ruth Gillespie Schuett (now Grooten-dorst). "I had never heard of the Blossomtime festival or St. Joseph as a matter of fact," said Witte, who resided then in Chicago. "But I had heard of the House of David baseball team—who hadn't? So I knew the general proximity of the parade."

The group assembled with the Gillespie family in front of Gillespie's Drug Store to watch the promenade down State Street. When a group of horses and riders wearing English hunt outfits and led by Caroline Dickinson Brown passed by, Witte mentioned that this was the English hunt seat he rode almost every Saturday on Chicago's bridal paths.

Ruth insisted that her son take Witte out to meet Brown. He did, and the couple was married about a year and a half later.

The Wittes honeymooned on the East coast and in Ber-muda. When they returned, Ruth invited them to dinner at the Green Cottage restaurant (now the site of the Glenn and Kathy Zerler residence). Also hosting the dinner party was Willis Stemm.

Ruth knew the society editor of the local newspaper and had mentioned to her that she and Stemm were giving a party for the newly married Wittes. When a photogra-pher arrived unannounced at the Green Cottage, the four dinner participants were surprised, but graciously obliged with the assignment.

When the paper ran a photograph of Lyle and Caroline Witte standing in front of a large floral centerpiece designed by Stemm, with a caption noting the occasion as a reception hosted by Schuett and Stemm, it caused quite a stir in town. For weeks afterward, people politely approached the Wittes and their hosts wondering why they had not been invited to the reception since they were such good friends.

Lyle Witte is the owner of Witte & Associates Interiors in St. Joseph. Carl Schuett is one of the associates in the business.

The Medical Degree of Joseph A. Hanley

Joe and Ruth Hanley entered the St. Joseph Sanitarium in 1946 for the birth of their first child, Carolyn Mackie. There were two nurses on duty and the Hanleys knew one of them, Joan Hosbein Rhinehardt.

Joan explained to the anxious parents that the only delivery room was already occupied. Ruth would have to be in surgery.

She also instructed Joe to put on a gown since it appeared there was going to be action very soon in both rooms and he might be called upon to help.

Joe telephoned Dr. Clayton Emery who surmised he was being summoned by a worried father and that there was no hurry. He was wrong. Little Carolyn was in a big hurry and delivery had started by the time Dr. Emery arrived. He was surprised and taken aback by Joe's presence in the delivery room as in those days only doctors and nurses participated in births. Dr. Emery told Joe that if he passed out they would simply ignore him and leave him on the floor.

Joe did not faint and when he walked out of surgery still wearing the gown, the other nurse saw him and immediately assumed he was a doctor. She called him Dr. Hanley from then on and he played along because this designation afforded him a few privileges such as open visitation.

This did backfire, however, when a woman just out of surgery was admitted into Ruth's room. The same nurse asked Joe if he would tend to her when she regained consciousness. He had no idea what to do other than hold her hand and wait. When she began to come around, Ruth told Joe to remove the tongue depressor from her mouth. When he did, he nearly fainted at the strong odor of ether on her breath and was in need of a doctor himself.

Joseph A. Hanley was a St. Joseph city commissioner for 16 years, and is the CEO of Vail Rubber Works, Inc. He has lived in St. Joseph for 68 years and says he's "one of many who believes St. Joseph is the greatest place to live."

Postscript: Carolyn's husband, Dick Mackie, has it on good authority that although the Hanleys produced other children Joe never again went into the delivery room.

Joe and Ruth Hanley

An Unusual Christmas Present

One Christmas season circa 1983, Tom Mance was hired by St. Joseph Today to portray Santa Claus. A very pretty young girl came into Santa's house on State Street and sat on Santa Tom's lap.

When they came to the part in their conversation where Santa asks "What do you want for Christmas?" Mance was deeply touched by her one and only request.

The little girl said she wanted a book on sign language.

When he asked her why, she replied, "A girl who is deaf has moved into my neighborhood and I want to be able to talk to her and become her friend."

Thomas Mance has lived in St. Joseph for 30 years. He is a past president of the Fairplain Lions Club and an associate at Sears.

Santa Tom

**Let's all start talking to each other
and become friends.**

Special thanks to all of our contributors:

Sharon Brightup Anstey
William Ast
Georgia Atwood
Nicholas G. Auringer
Bruce & Margie Ball
Joe Bartz
Mary Baske
Lila & Joseph Blake
Dr. Walter F. Browe
Gladys Eisenhart-Brown
Priscilla Upton Byrns
Jim & June Caldwell
Nancy & Allen Cassada
Marjorie S. Clemens
Edward J. Conrad
Dawn Consolino
Jean Dalzell
H. Thomas Dewhirst
Phyllis Dowsett
Inez R. Dumke
Maggie Dumke
Barbara C. Durflinger
Clifford R. Emlong
Lewis L. Filstrup
Ted Fleisher
A. Karl Gast
Dr. Emery George
Dottie Ruggles Gietler
Robert Gillespie
William G. Gillespie
George Glade
Eileen Globensky
John Globensky

Ruth Gillespie Grootendorst
Virginia Handy
Joseph A. Hanley
Irma F. Harris
Martha & Joseph P. "Porky" Harvey
Ron Heyn
Sally & Edward Hoffmann
Dale C. Hogue
John E.N. & Dede Howard
Ida Jager
Paul Johnson
Virginia Johnson
Elowyn Ann Keech
George S. Keller
Robert A. Ketelhut
Allen Klemm
Frank Klemm
Jean Schuett Koebel
Elsie Kesterke Kolberg
Frank F. Lahr
Elizabeth Landis
Sandra Landis
Bradford Laughlin
Georgia Hill Leonard
Mrs. Felix (Margaret Schreiber) Leonarduzzi
Kenneth John Leonarduzzi
Fred & Alberta Longner
Ted & Elaine Lucker
Mrs. Arthur F. (Leona) Ludwig
Thomas E. & Elenore Lyons
Thomas Mance
Gary E. McCormick
Pat & Alan McKee
Marion McKenna
P.J. "Pat" McMullen

William Mihalik
Chuck & Doris Miller
Patrick M. Moody
Robert C. Orlaske
Marilyn Pape
Polly Preston Parrett
Mary C. "Lee" Passaro
Miriam Pede
Marilyn Peterson
Stephen & Delores "Dee" Reagan
Rosemary Ritter
Thomas & Mary Robbins
Pasquale & Anna Santaniello
Gwenn Ueck Schadler
Dr. Paula M. Schlenzka
Dan Schnitta
Ardys J. Schultz
Louis C. Schultz
Warren Seabury
Robert P. Small
Duke Sparks
Tom Sparks
William E. Swisher
Ronald J. Taylor
Templin's Music & Electronics
Roberta Drake Terrill
Phyllis Thurkettle
Thelma Troost
Amey Upton
Elaine C. Vanderberg
Marge Wiatrowski
Lyle C. Witte
Glenn L. Zerler
Babe Zollar